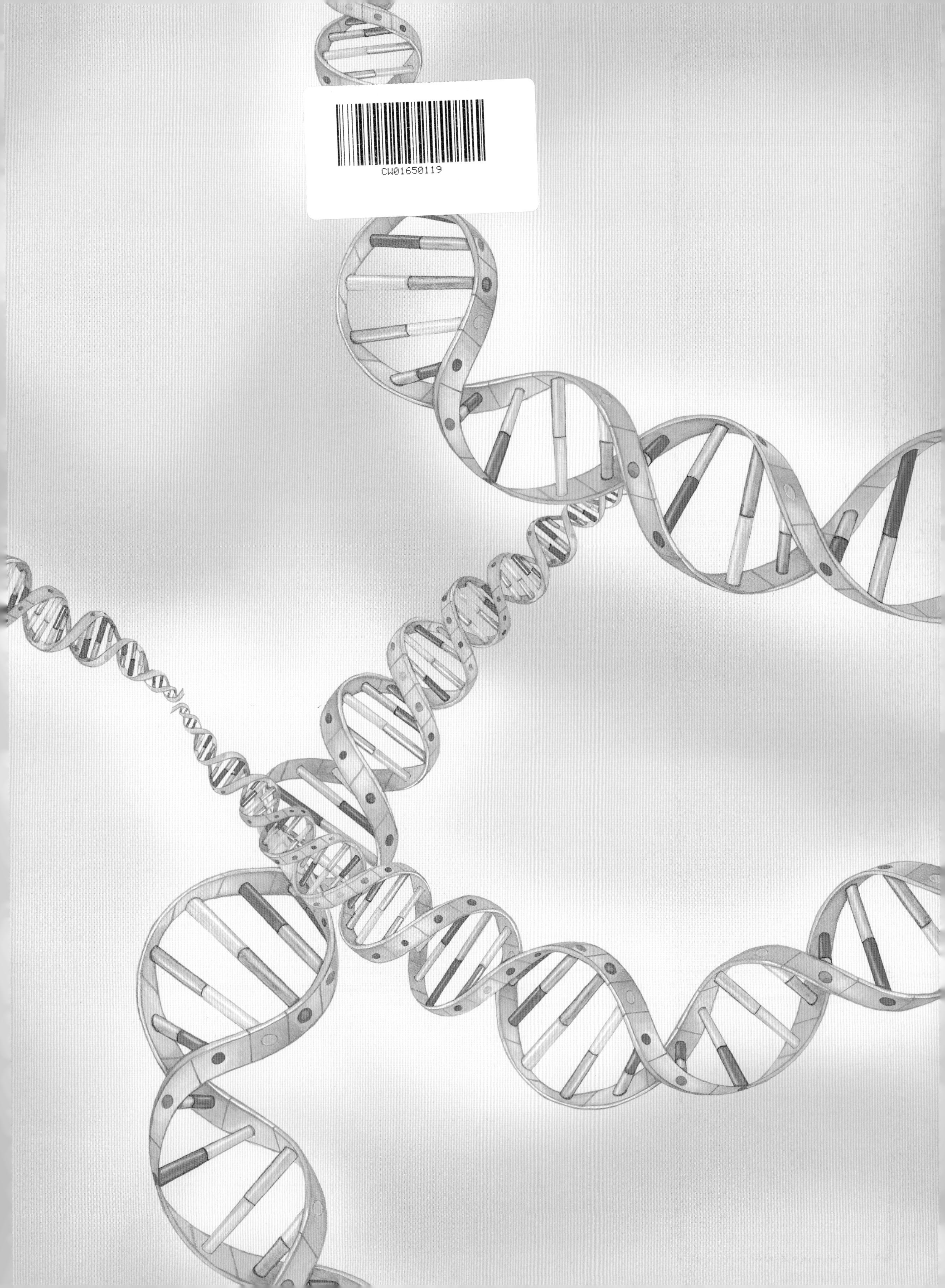

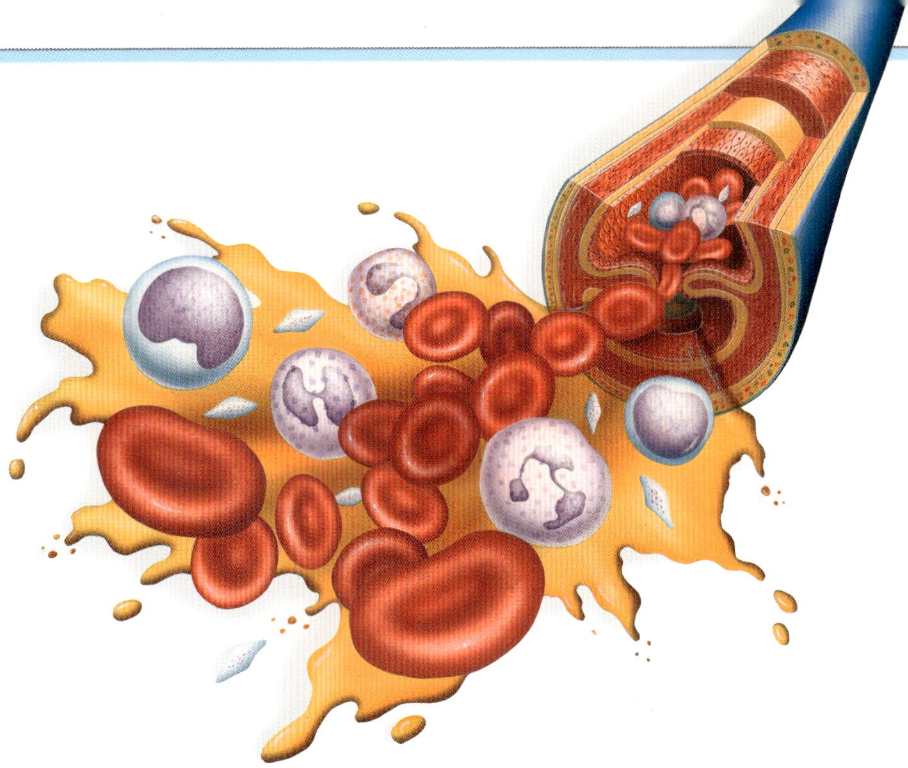

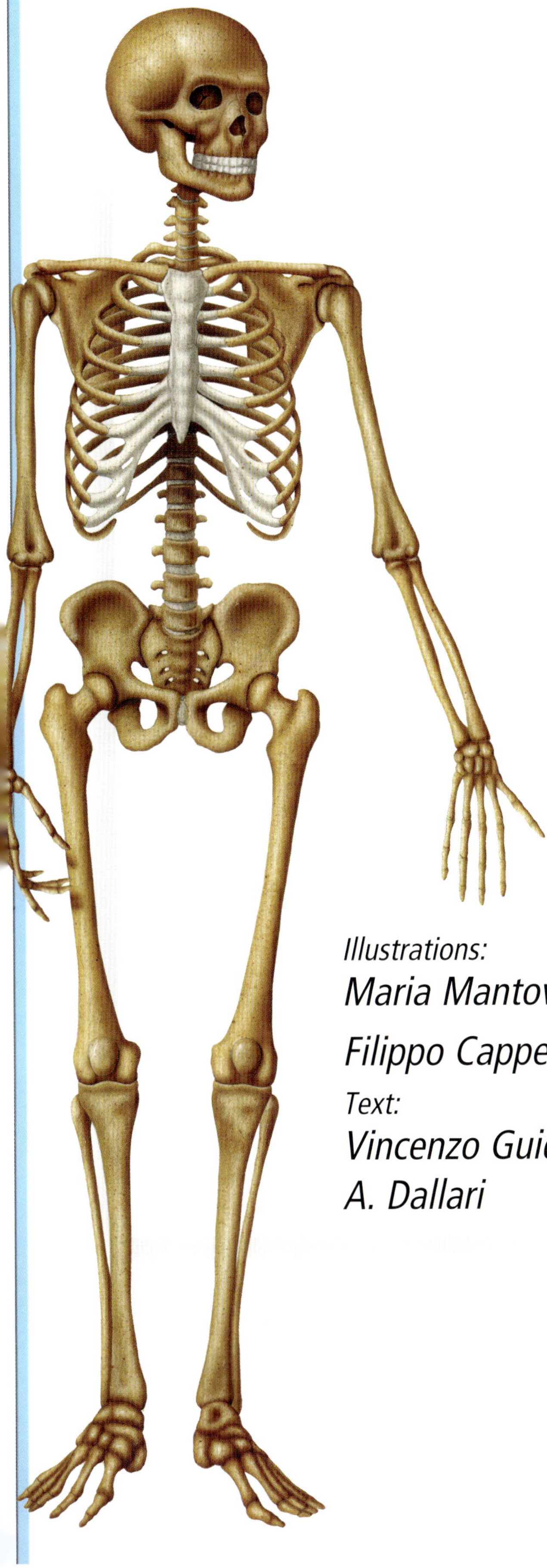

THE HUMAN BODY

A Journey of Discovery

Illustrations:
Maria Mantovani
Filippo Cappelli
Text:
Vincenzo Guidi
A. Dallari

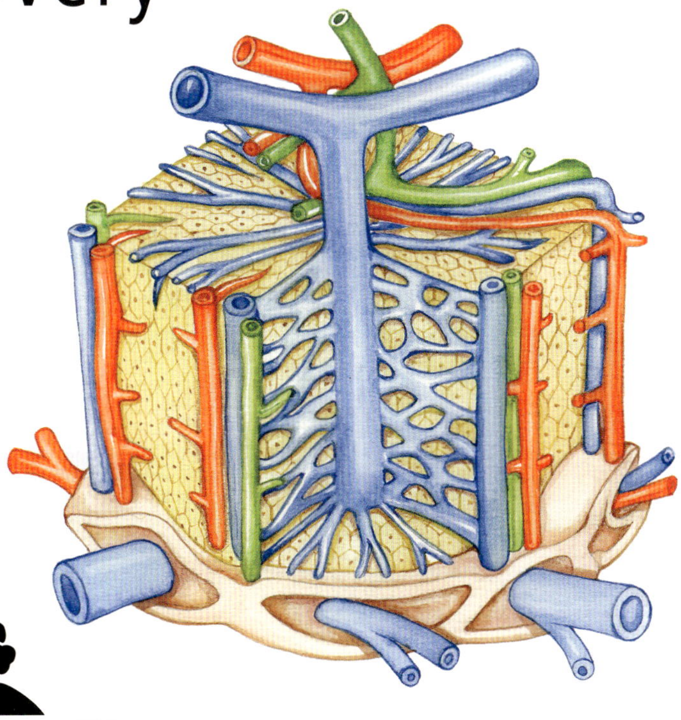

The Five Mile Press

This edition published by
The Five Mile Press Pty Ltd
950 Stud Road, Rowville
Victoria 3178 Australia
Email: publishing@fivemile.com.au
Website: www.fivemile.com.au

Cover design: Diana Vlad
English translation: Lorraine David
Medical and science consultant for this edition: Calvin Miller

This English language edition first published 2007

National Library of Australia Cataloguing-in-Publication data:
Guidi, Vincenzo.
The human body.

English ed.
Includes index.
For primary school students aged 8 and over.
ISBN 9781741784695.

1. Body, Human - Juvenile literature. 2. Anatomy - Juvenile literature. I. Dallari, A. II. Title.

611

Printed in China 5 4 3 2 1

CONTENTS

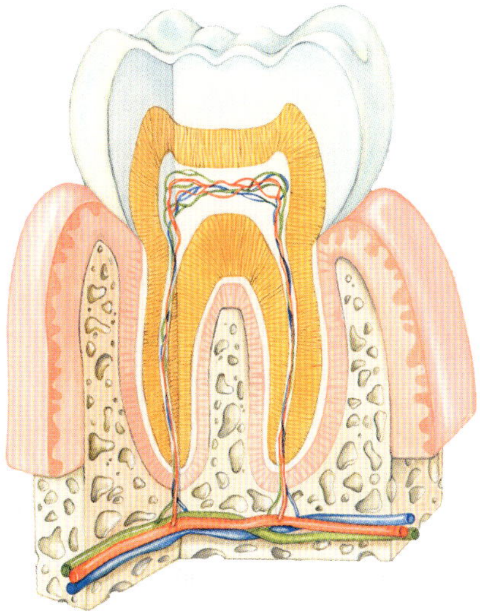

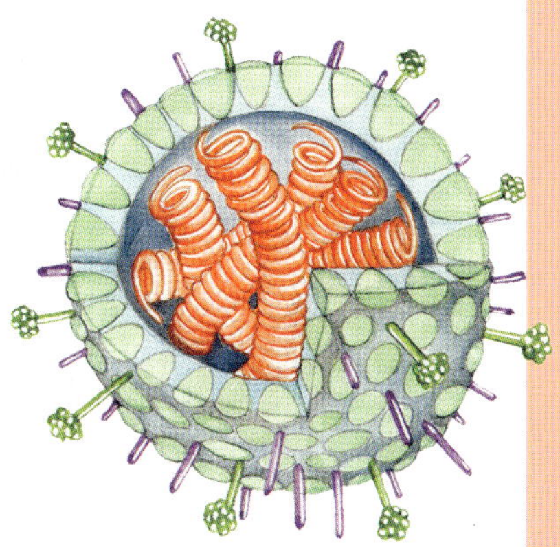

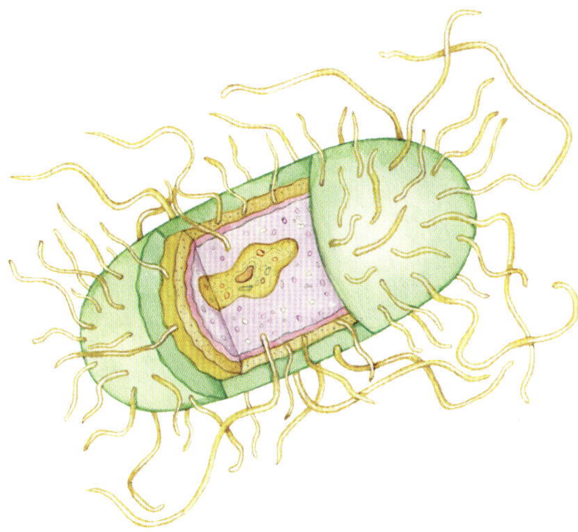

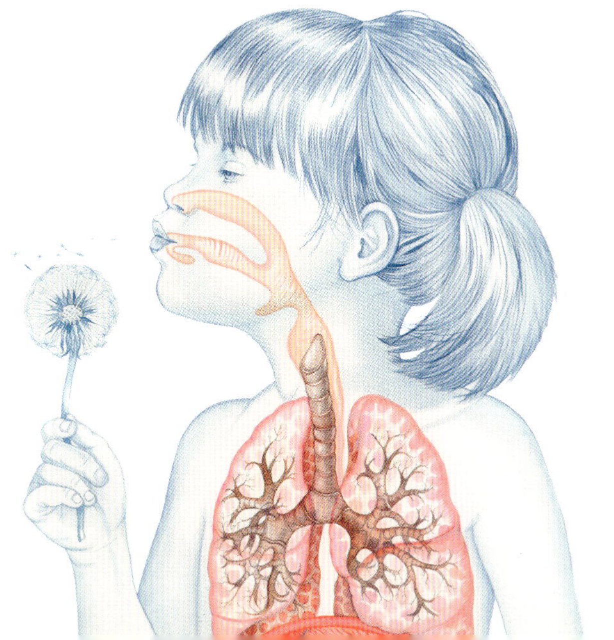

CELLS and DNA

The most basic unit in the human body is the cell. Billions of these tiny structures work together in harmony to ensure that the human body functions correctly. Each cell is wrapped in an outer membrane which protects it from the surrounding environment. Inside the cell is the cytoplasm. This is a jelly-like material containing a number of substances and organelles. In the centre of each cell is a nucleus, which contains the chromosomes carrying the genes in molecules called DNA.

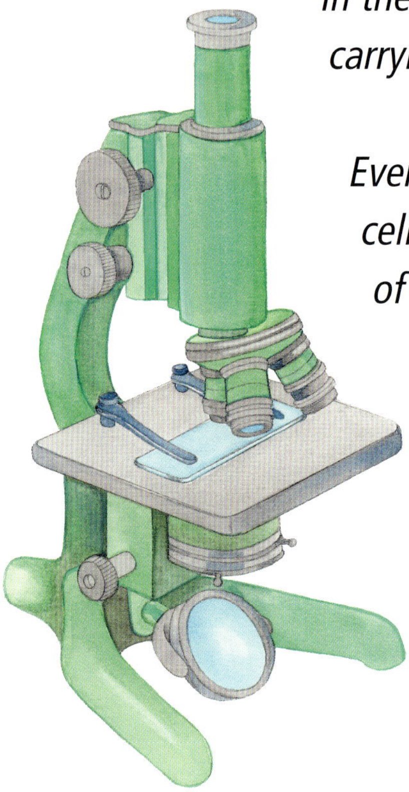

Every cell in our body derives from a cell that was formed at the moment of our conception. Each cell has the ability to divide, thus forming two identical copies. It is this division of cells that allows us to grow.

Cell dimensions

Cells are minute and are not visible to the naked eye. A drop of blood contains millions of red blood cells which each measure only a few thousandths of a millimetre. Nerve cells, and the cells of women's ova, grow much bigger than that. Cells are complex organisms which need to be nourished and which then eliminate the waste produced by their activity. The vacuoles located in their outer membrane facilitate this dual role.

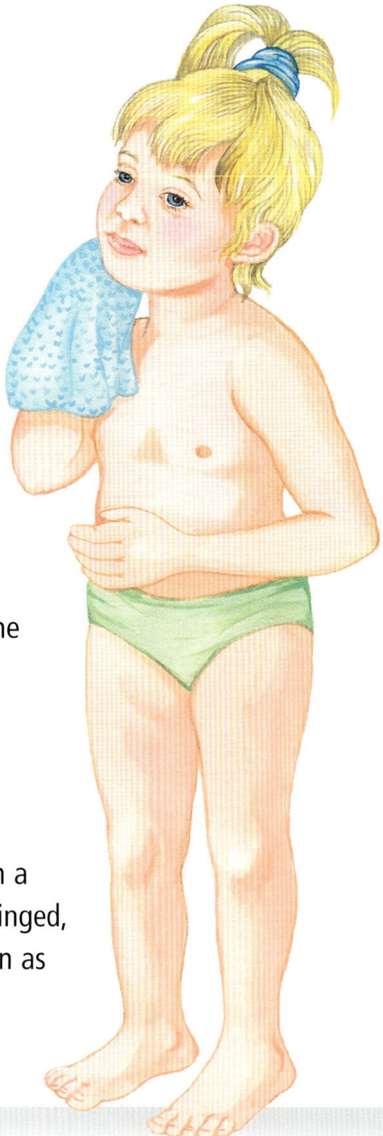

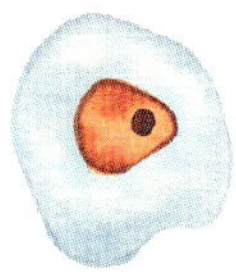

Skin

Skin cells (epithethial cells) are very close to one another and form tissues that cover the whole body.

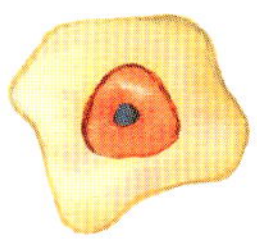

Fat

Fat reserves accumulate inside the adipose cells and tend to crush the nucleus.

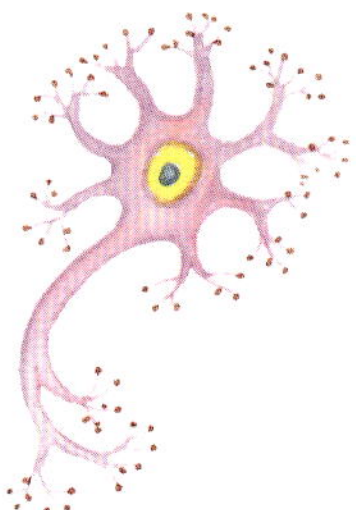

Nerves

Nerve cells (neurons) contain a long axon ending in many fringed, branch-like extensions known as dendrites.

Bones

Bone tissue cells are contained in a solid, shapeless substance.

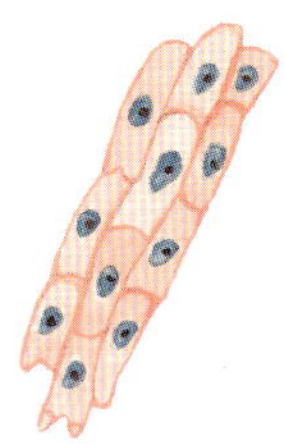

Muscles

Muscle cells have an elongated shape and are arranged into bundles which are capable of expanding and contracting.

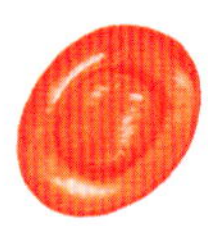

Blood

Red blood cells are circular in shape and concave in the centre. Although small, they transport large quantities of haemoglobin. Red blood cells are the only cells that don't have a nucleus.

Nucleus

The nucleus of a cell is surrounded by a membrane full of holes. This protection isolates the DNA molecules from the cytoplasm around it. Genetic material is stored in filaments called chromatin. Inside the Golgi apparatus, proteins and fats are modified for export outside of the cell.

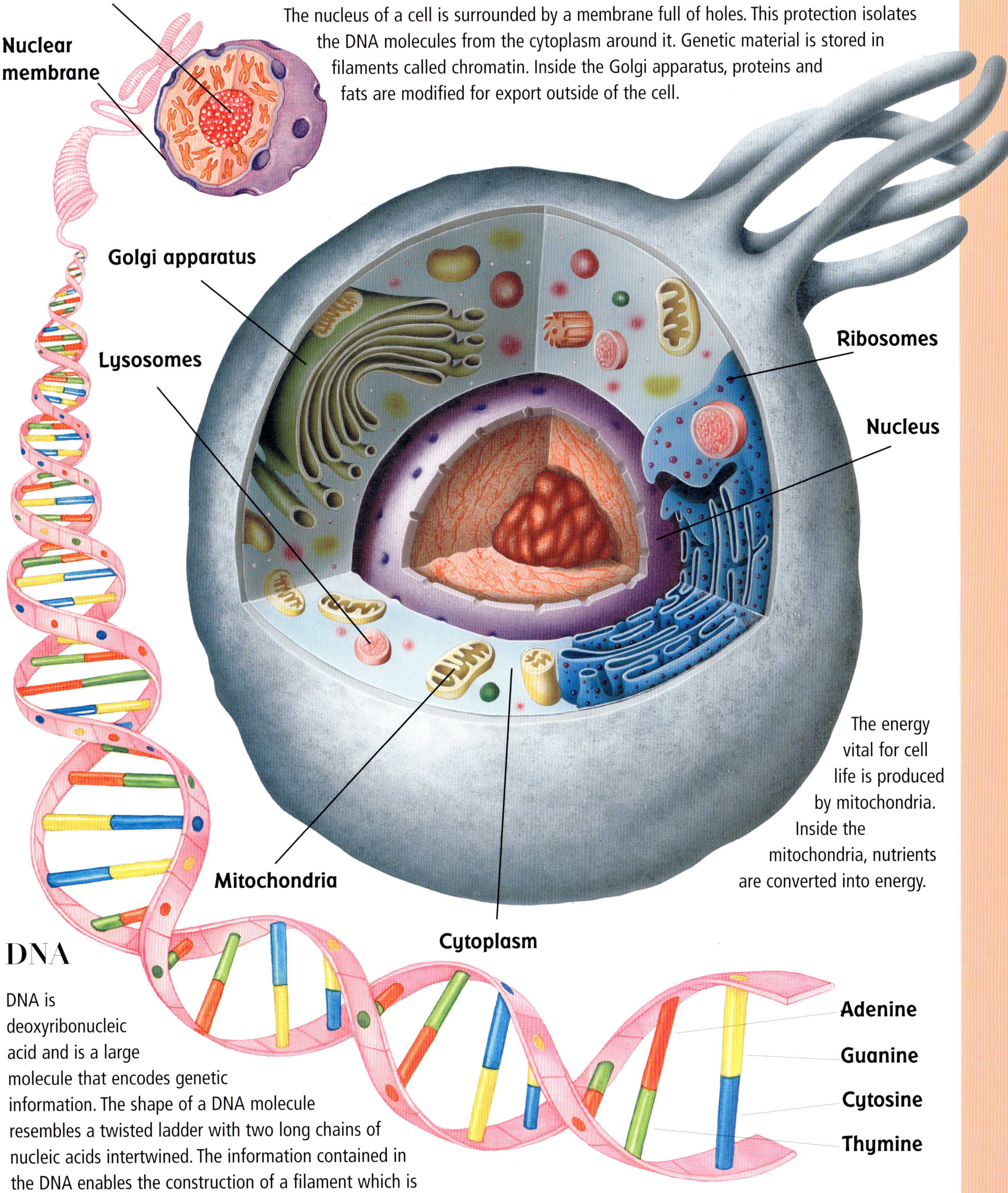

The energy vital for cell life is produced by mitochondria. Inside the mitochondria, nutrients are converted into energy.

DNA

DNA is deoxyribonucleic acid and is a large molecule that encodes genetic information. The shape of a DNA molecule resembles a twisted ladder with two long chains of nucleic acids intertwined. The information contained in the DNA enables the construction of a filament which is genetically identical, complete, and capable of ensuring continued life. DNA segments, known as genes, control cell activity.

THE VITAL ORGANS

The human body is made up of basic units called cells, of which there are more than 300 distinct types. Together, these millions of cells form tissues. Different types of tissues form our various organs.

All the vital organs, except for the brain, are contained in the trunk. This large part of the human body consists of two cavities which are separated by a muscle called the diaphragm. In the upper part is the heart and the two lungs. The thoracic cage and ribs are wrapped around these delicate organs to protect them. The lower part of the trunk contains the organs related to the digestive, urinary and reproductive systems.

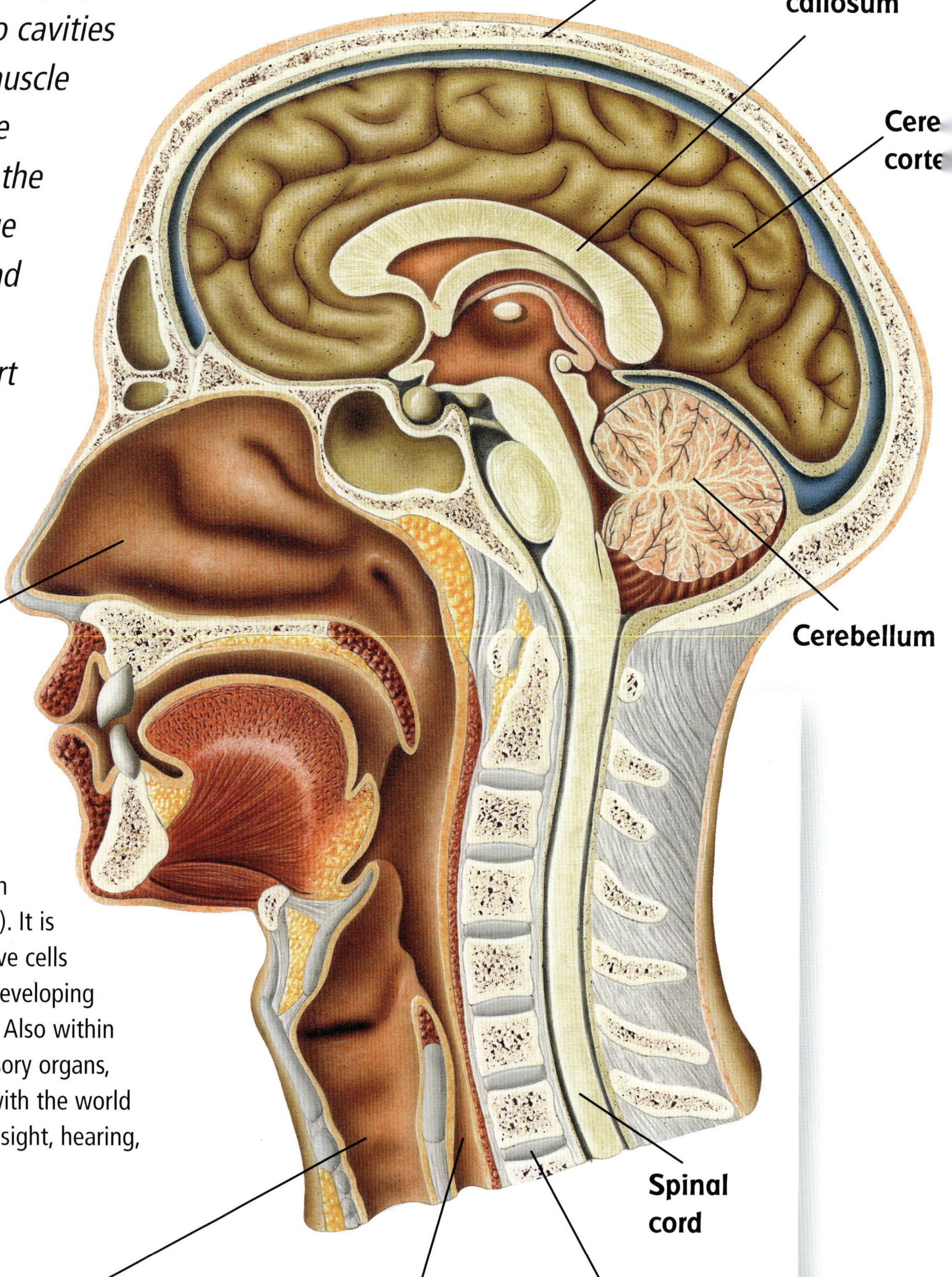

The head

The head contains the most complex organ in the human body: the brain (encephalon). It is formed from 100 billion nerve cells called neurons, capable of developing our most complex thoughts. Also within the head are important sensory organs, which allow us to interact with the world around us via our senses of sight, hearing, smell, taste and touch.

Systems

A group of organs that work together to carry out their functions is referred to as a system. Each system is responsible for a vital function. The main systems in the human body are the digestive system, the cardiovascular system, the respiratory system, the endocrine and lymphatic systems, the reproductive system, the nervous system and the musculoskeletal system.

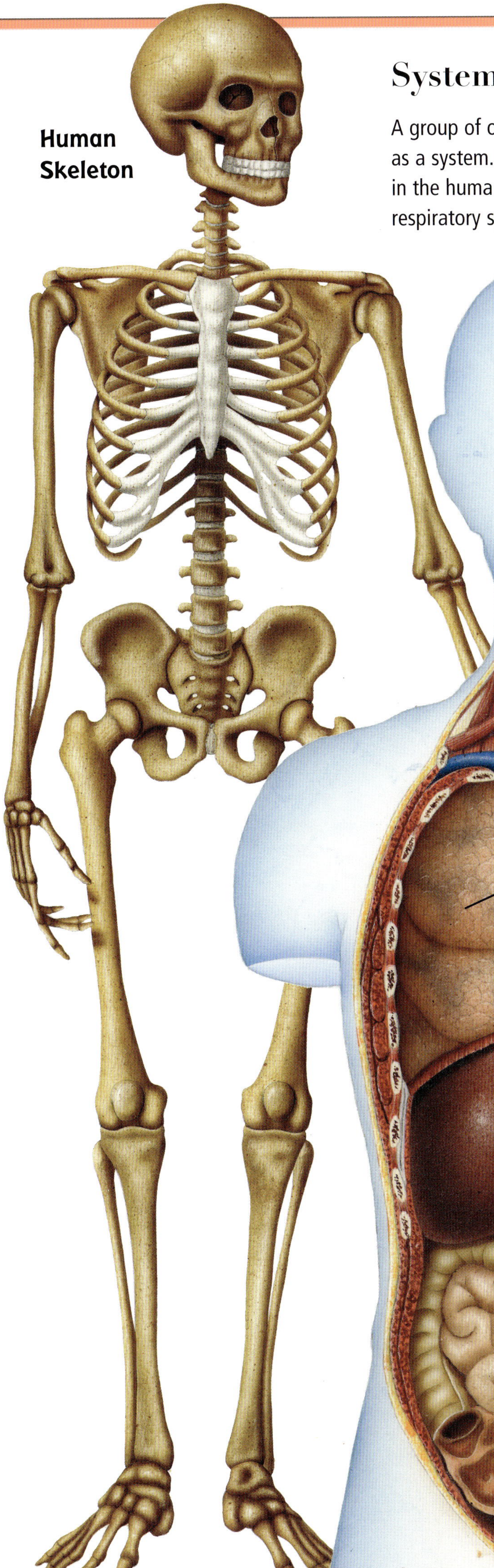

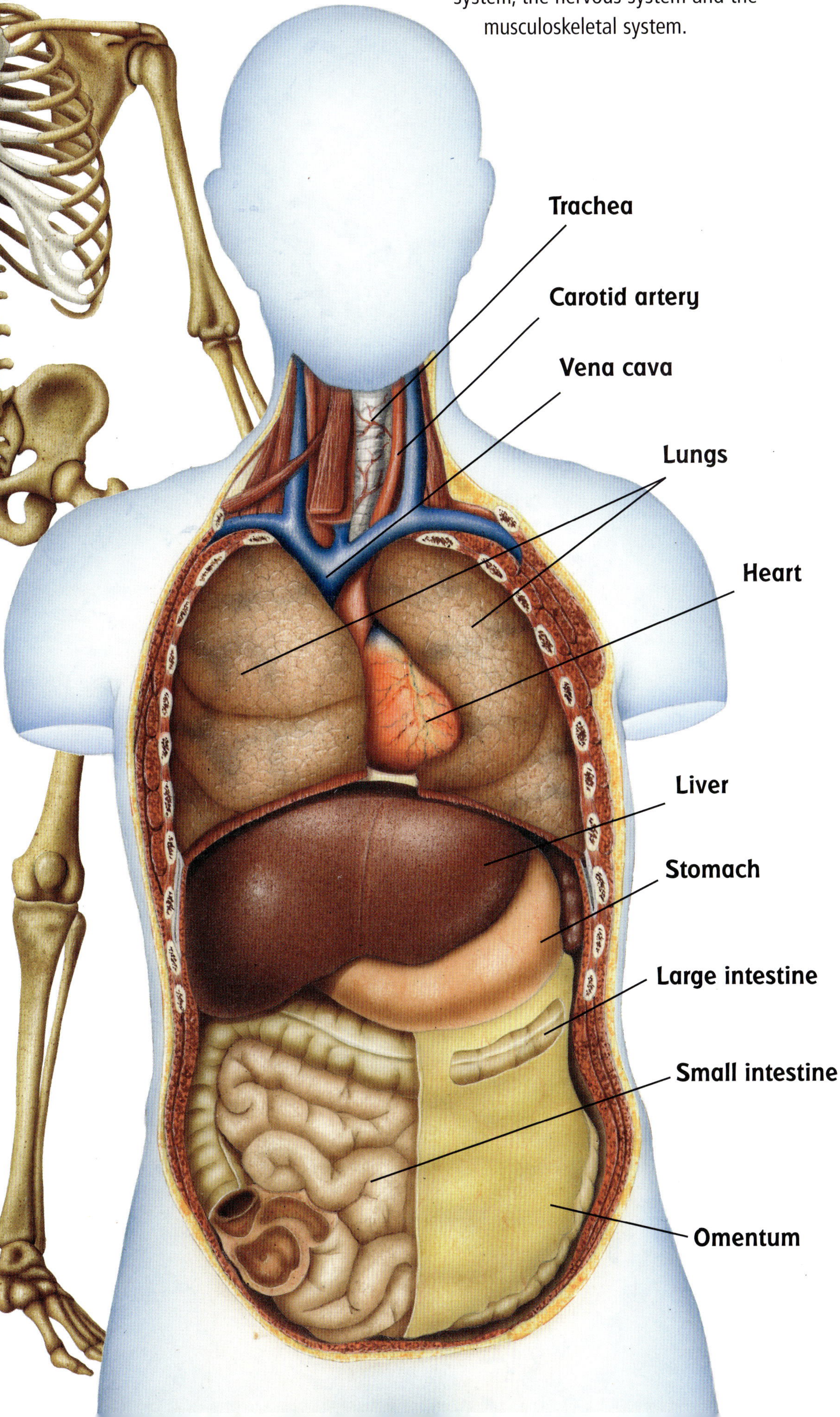

THE SKELETON

The skeleton is the framework which supports our body. Its rigid structure supports our muscles and protects our internal organs.

The skeleton consists of 206 bones and pieces of cartilage, which are held in the correct position by strips of tissue called ligaments. The whole skeleton is made up of two parts.

The first is the axial skeleton consisting of the cranium, spine and thoracic cage. The second is the appendicular skeleton, which consists of the upper and lower limbs, and the scapular and pelvic girdles.

Bone tissue

Bone tissue is rich in mineral salts, which makes the bones strong and rigid. In children, the concentration of salts is lower than in the completely formed bones of adults. That is why very young children are especially supple and can move their bodies in ways that would be impossible for older people.

Bones are made of a tissue that appears to be static, but which is continually changing. Inside our bones, old tissue is broken down and released into the bloodstream as salts, while new bone tissue is formed. This process continues all through our lifetime. There are three different types of bones, distinguished according to their shape: flat bones (like those in the head), long bones

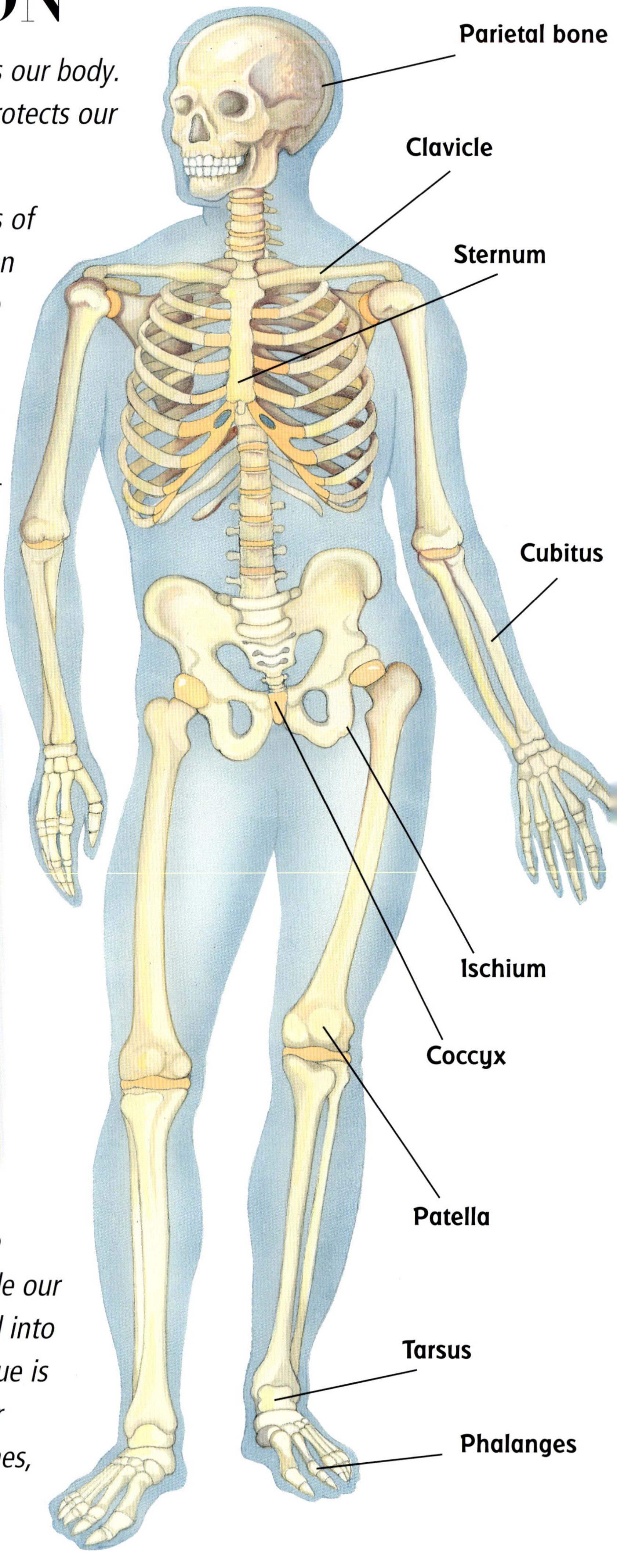

(like those in the arms and legs) and short bones (like those found in the hands). All are formed from bone tissue, which is rich in tiny cells contained within a hard framework. If we look at a cross-section of a bone, we can see it consists of thin slivers arranged in layers around small channels with veins and tiny arteries running through them.

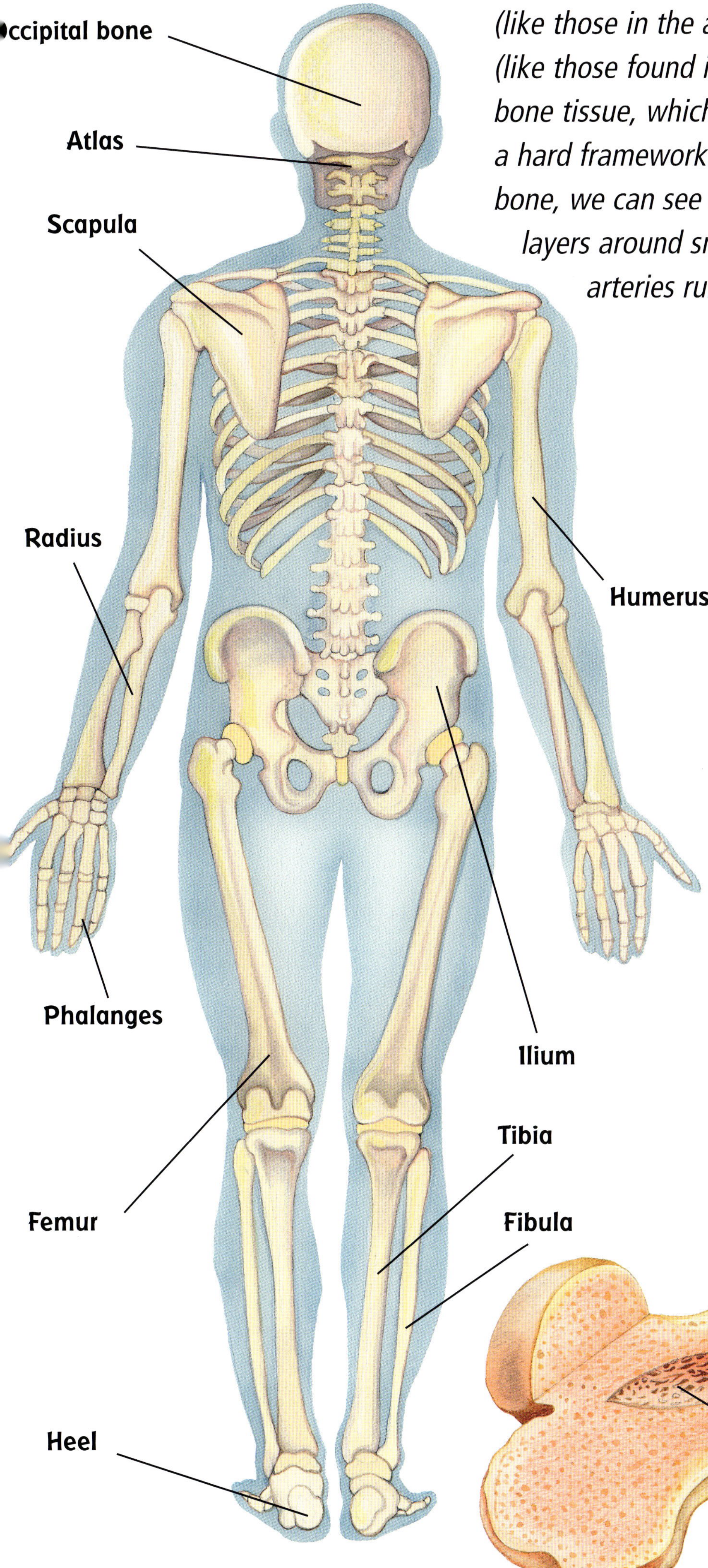

Bone marrow

The deep, spongy part inside certain bones is a tissue called the marrow, which is able to manufacture both red and white blood cells. Large amounts of marrow are found in the femur, pelvis, sternum and skull.

Blood cells need to be produced continually because their life span is rather short, and they must be replaced.

Inside certain long bones is another kind of marrow, which stores excess reserves of fat and minerals.

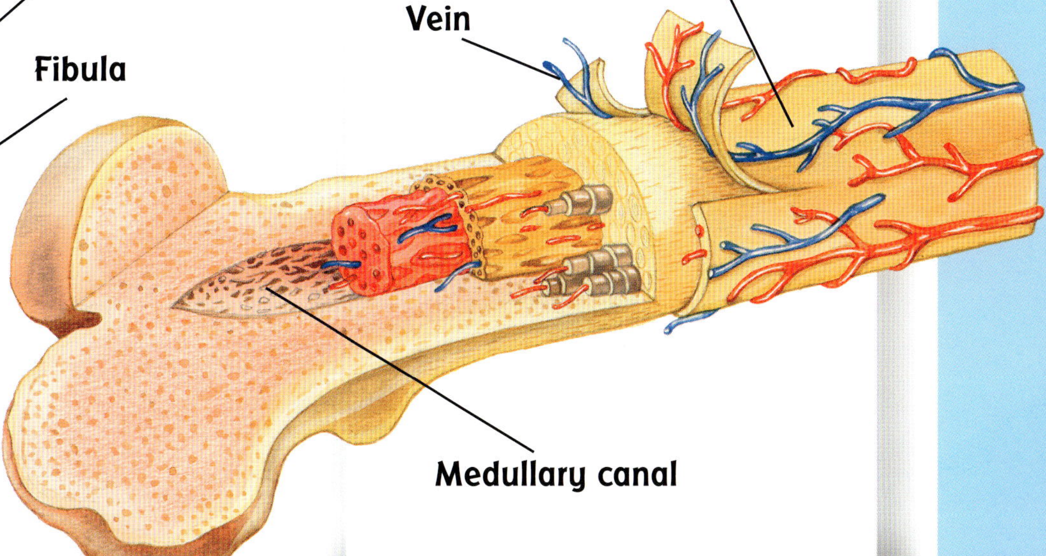

THE SKULL

The set of bones forming the head is referred to as the skull (cranium). These bones have a light but particularly strong structure, which is specially adapted to protect the internal parts of the head. They are made up of two distinct and compact layers. In between is a layer of spongy matter containing a dense network of cavities and nerves.

The various bones of the cranium are fixed together into rigid joints which hold them in place. The only moving parts of the skull are the lower jaw (mandible) and the joint between the head and the neck, called the first cervical vertebra.

Cranium

The cranium is made up of 29 different bones, including six inside the ears and one underneath the base of the tongue. The brain is protected by the cranium, which is formed from eight curved bones fixed together.

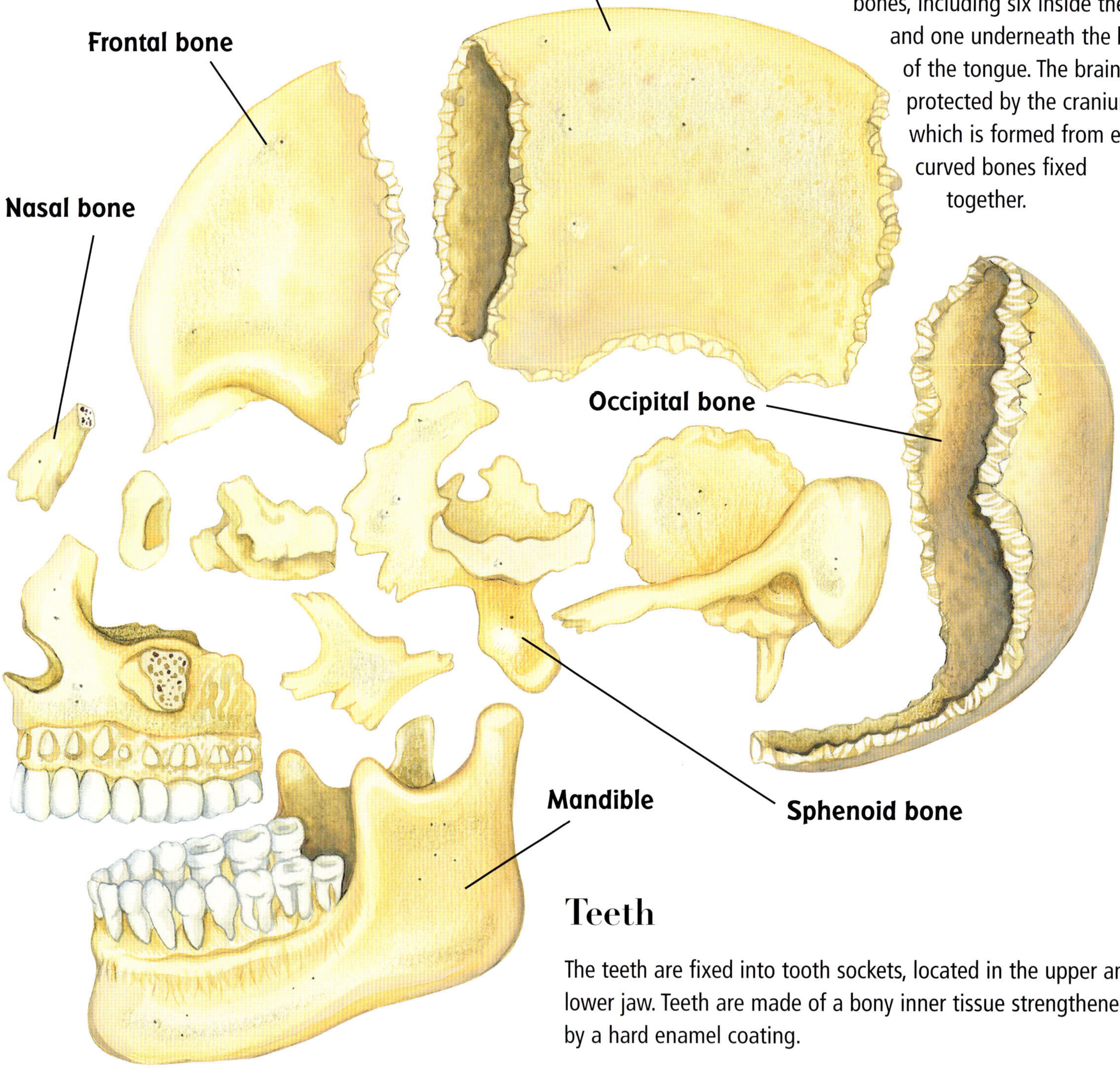

Teeth

The teeth are fixed into tooth sockets, located in the upper and lower jaw. Teeth are made of a bony inner tissue strengthened by a hard enamel coating.

Helmets

Whenever there is a risk of severe impact to the head, it is always advisable to wear a helmet for increased protection. Specific helmets are available for cycling, motorcycling and other sports. Special helmets are also manufactured for military use or for those working in dangerous environments.

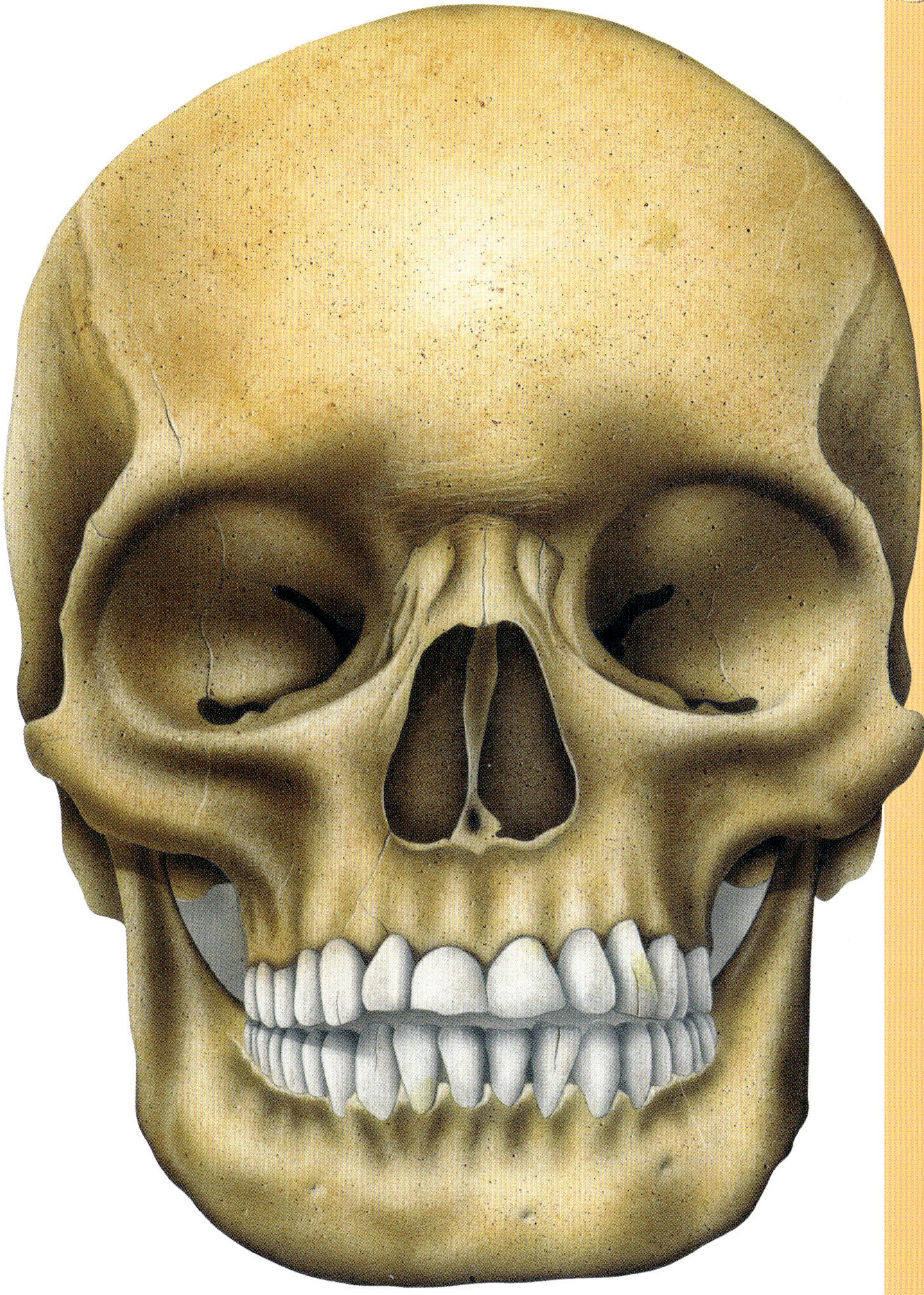

The cranial capacity of modern adult humans varies from 1500 cubic centimetres to 1800 cubic centimetres.

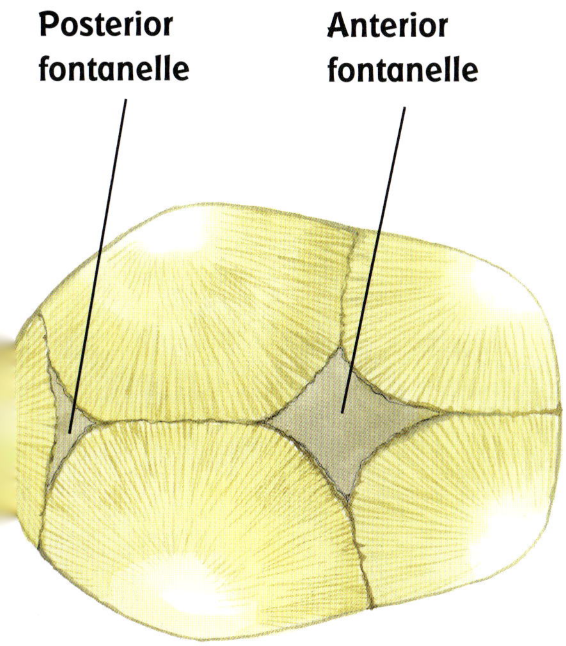

Skull of a newborn infant

In newborns, the cranial bones are not fused together. A newborn has six different cranial sections, which are protected simply by membranes. These are gradually replaced by sutures of connective tissue. These areas are particularly elastic so that the skull remains flexible and can adapt more easily to the various stages of the birth process.

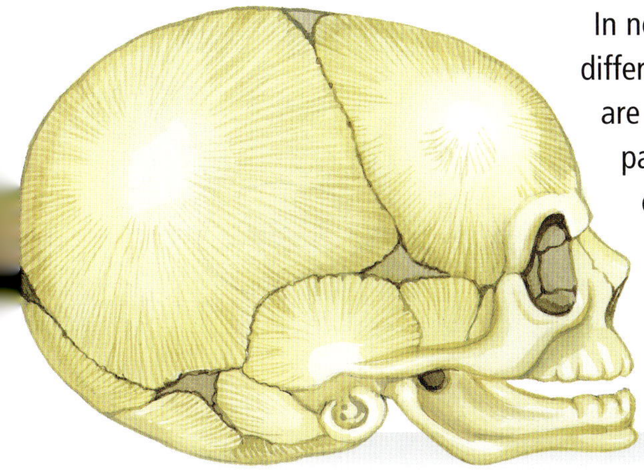

THE THORAX AND PELVIS

The thoracic cage is a bony, protective shell which houses the heart and lungs. It is made up of 12 pairs of ribs joined at the rear to the spinal vertebrae. At the front, inside the chest, 10 pairs of ribs are attached to the breast bone (sternum), which is a flat bone formed of three segments. The two lower pairs hang freely and are not attached at the front.

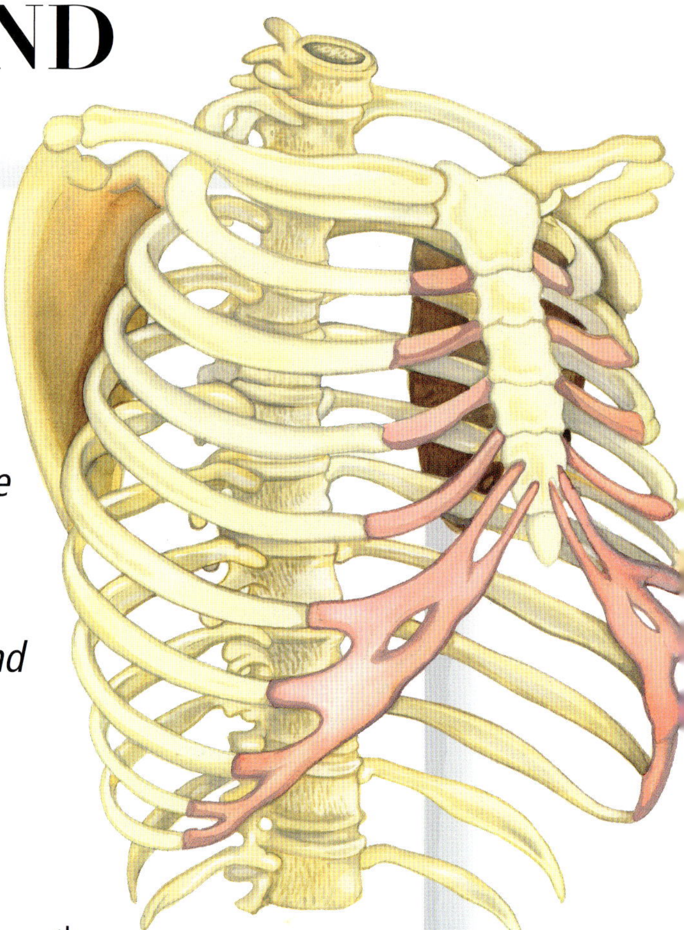

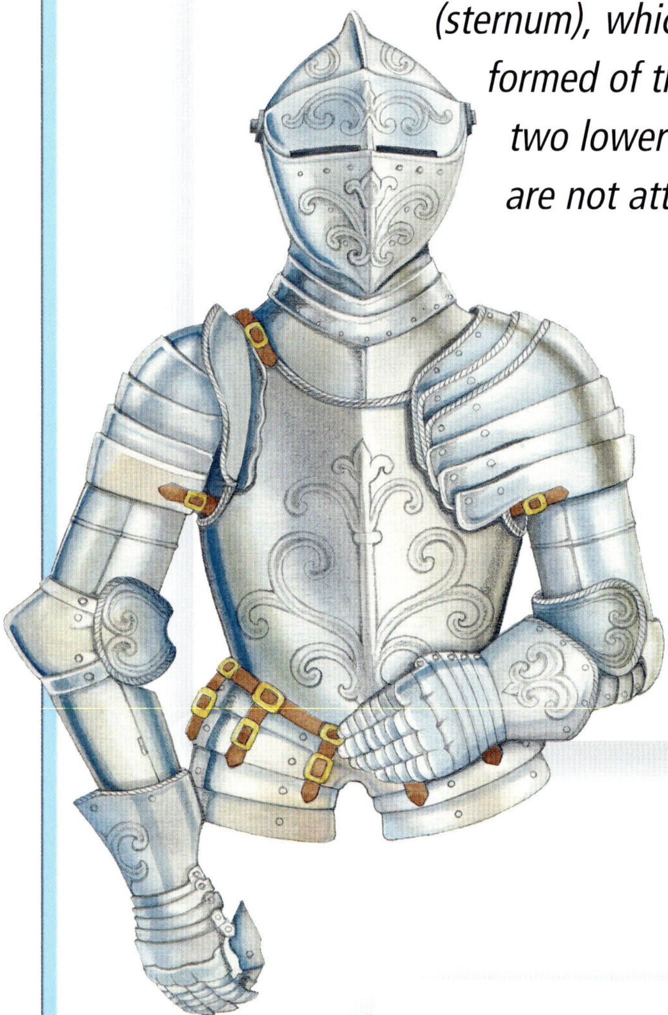

The head and the trunk are the two most vulnerable parts of the human body. In bygone times, warriors wore metal armour for greater protection of their internal organs. Breastplates and helmets were frequently used on ancient battlefields to protect against harmful blades and spears.

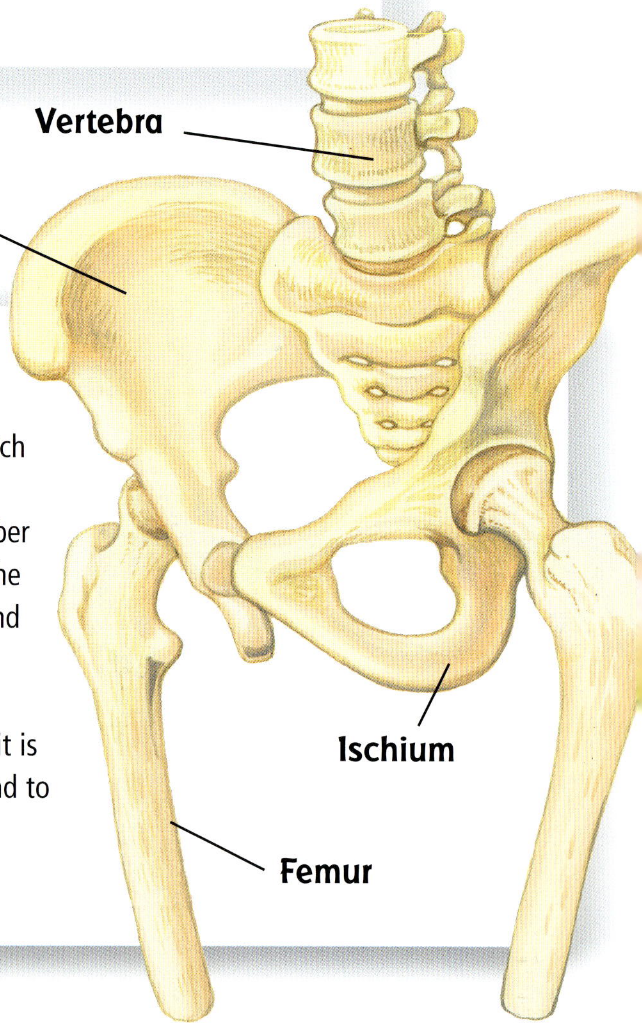

Pelvis

The pelvis is a bony, basin-shaped receptacle, which shelters the organs of the lower abdomen and supports the upper leg joints. It comprises a number of bony parts: the two hips, which are joined to the spine at the sacrum; and the ilium, the ischium and the pubis, which are three bones fused together.

The female pelvis is larger than that of males, as it is designed to shelter the fetus during pregnancy and to facilitate the birthing process.

THE SPINE

The spine is a long vertical structure, which supports the human body. It is formed from separate vertebrae and allows us to move with flexibility and to stand upright. Thus, we can bend sideways and rotate our torso in relation to our feet.

The vertebrae are made of bony tissue, and in the spaces between each one are discs of cartilage that absorb the pressures of compression or tension caused by movement.

The spine is divided into five parts: the cervical area involving the vertebrae which support the head, the thoracic area to which the ribs are attached, the lumbar area consisting of five vertebrae, the sacral area formed from five vertebrae joined to the sacrum and, finally, the coccyx (the small bone at the very base of the spine).

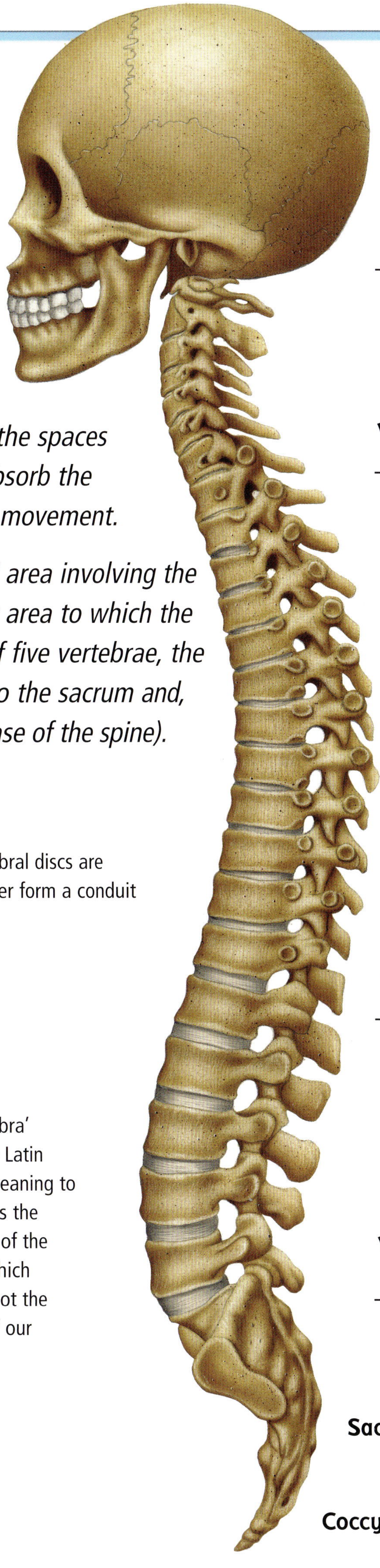

Vertebrae

Each vertebra has a hole through the rear section. All the vertebral discs are superimposed one on top of the other, and all the holes together form a conduit inside which the spinal cord is housed.

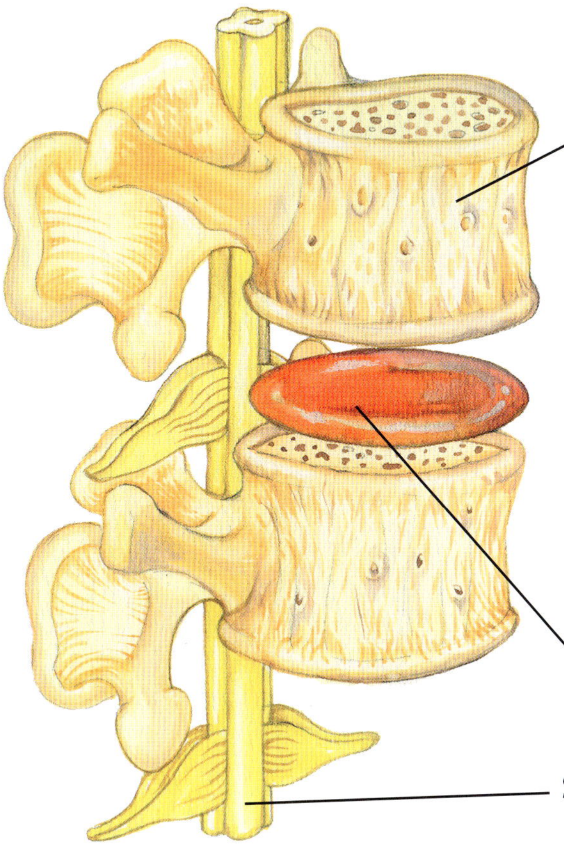

The word 'vertebra' comes from the Latin verb 'vertere' meaning to turn. It describes the specific feature of the human spine which allows us to pivot the trunk section of our skeleton.

THE JOINTS

The point where two or more bones meet is called a joint. When the two bones are locked rigidly together, this is referred to as a suture. If the bones are able to move independently, it is a mobile joint. All bone surfaces are covered with a slippery cartilage to facilitate movement.

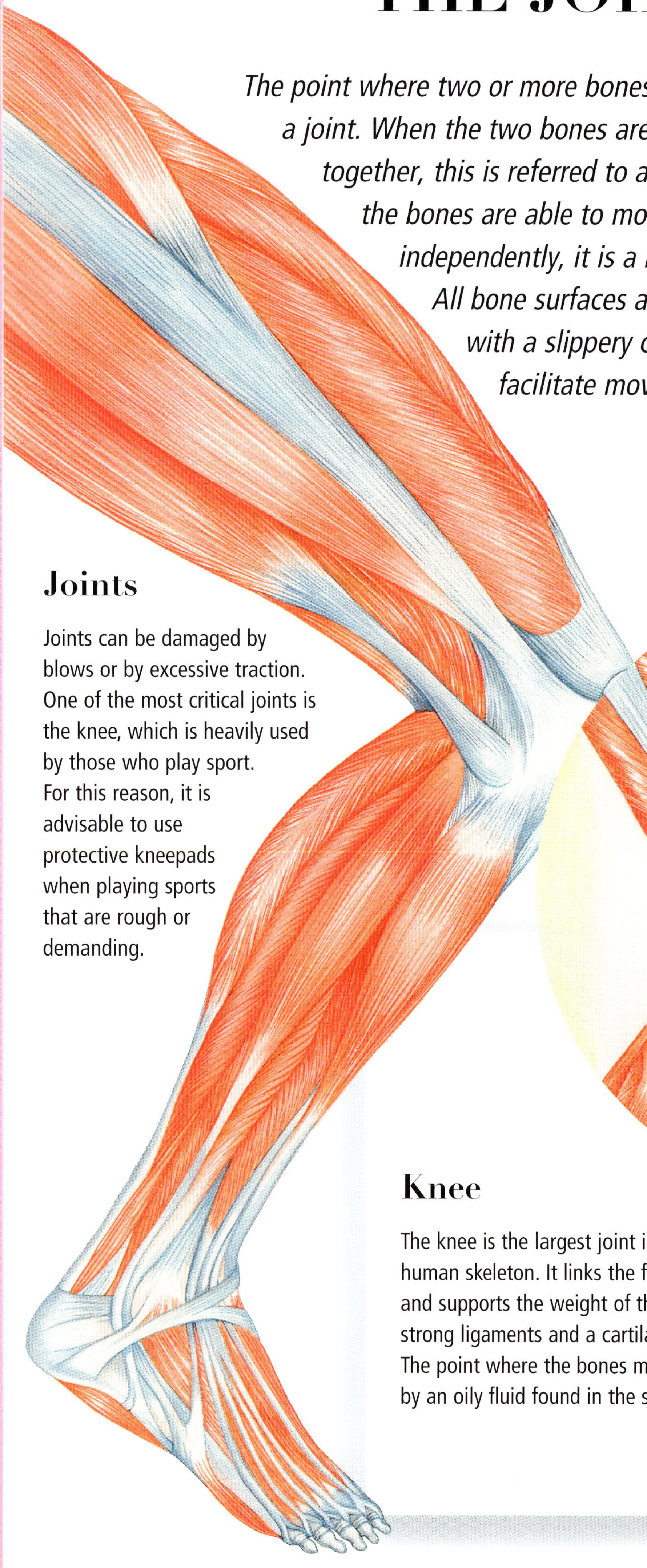

Joints

Joints can be damaged by blows or by excessive traction. One of the most critical joints is the knee, which is heavily used by those who play sport. For this reason, it is advisable to use protective kneepads when playing sports that are rough or demanding.

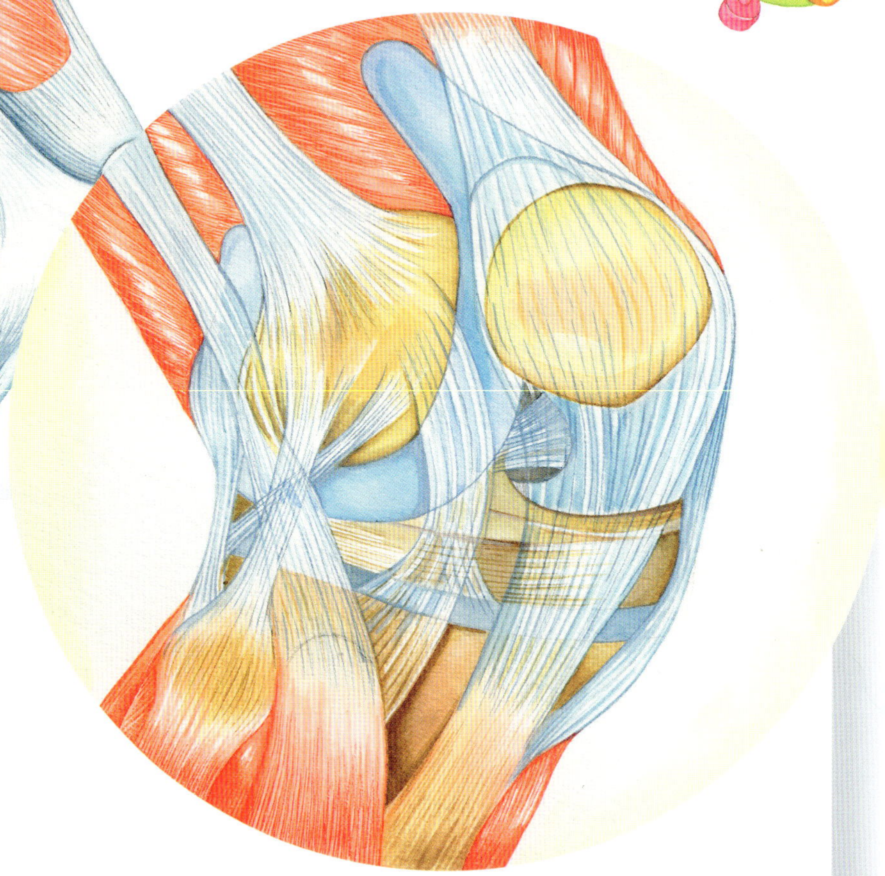

Knee

The knee is the largest joint in the human skeleton. It links the femur to the tibia and supports the weight of the whole body. Its structure is reinforced by four very strong ligaments and a cartilage called the meniscus, which stabilises the joint. The point where the bones meet is subject to constant friction, and is lubricated by an oily fluid found in the synovial membrane.

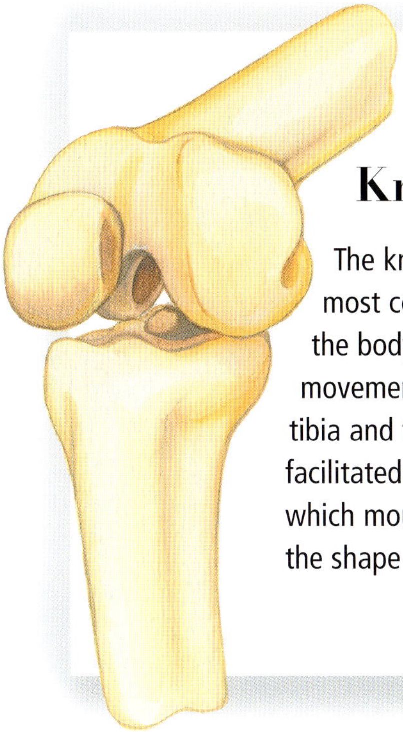

Knee

The knee is one of the most complex joints in the body. Sliding movement between the tibia and the femur is facilitated by the meniscus, which moulds the tibia to fit the shape of the femur.

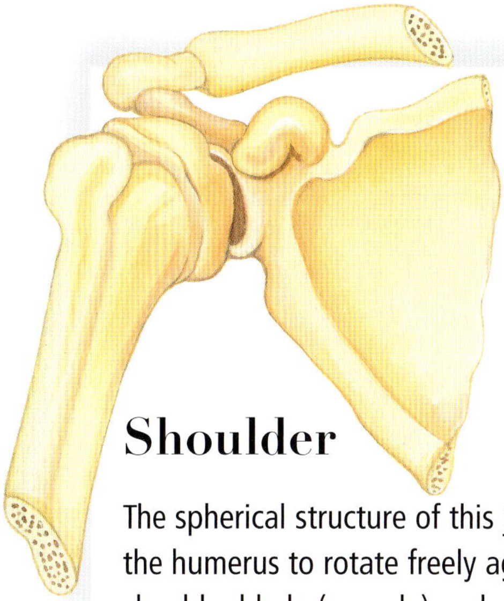

Shoulder

The spherical structure of this joint allows the humerus to rotate freely against the shoulder blade (scapula) and allows a wide range of movements.

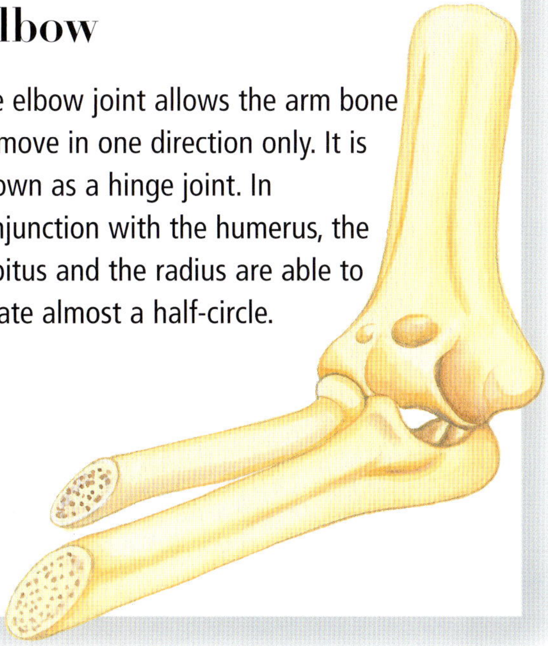

Elbow

The elbow joint allows the arm bone to move in one direction only. It is known as a hinge joint. In conjunction with the humerus, the cubitus and the radius are able to rotate almost a half-circle.

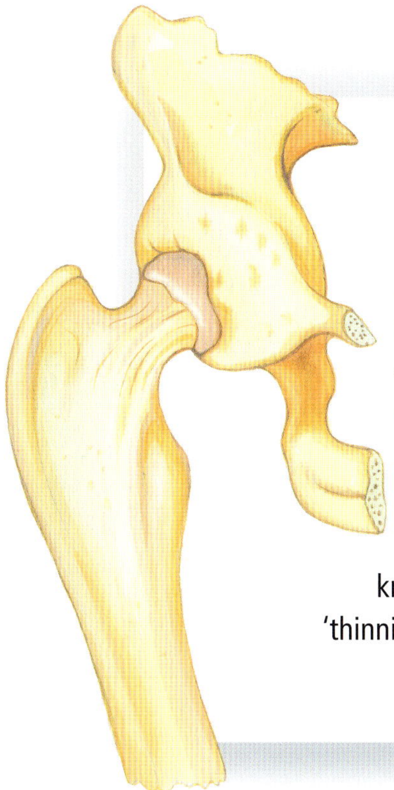

Hip

The head of the femur is connected to the pelvis by a spherical ball joint, which allows it to move very freely. This joint is especially subject to injury in people suffering from the disorder known as osteoporosis, or 'thinning of the bones'.

All joints are covered with a tough, smooth elastic tissue known as cartilage. It allows the joint to withstand mechanical forces and provides a smooth surface for movement.

Ligaments are fibrous bands which tie the ends of bones securely together at the joints. They are made of a very strong, elastic connective tissue with a fibrous structure. Despite these qualities, the ligaments are still one of the weakest parts of the skeletal system.

SKELETAL MUSCLES

More than 600 skeletal muscles allow movement of bones in all parts of the body. They make up approximately half of our body weight and help to link our various bones together. They are composed from a single cell type known as skeletal muscle fibre. These fibres are able to change their length by contracting. This action allows them to shorten their length by half, compared to when the muscle is at rest. During contraction, strength develops in proportion to the number of muscle fibres involved.

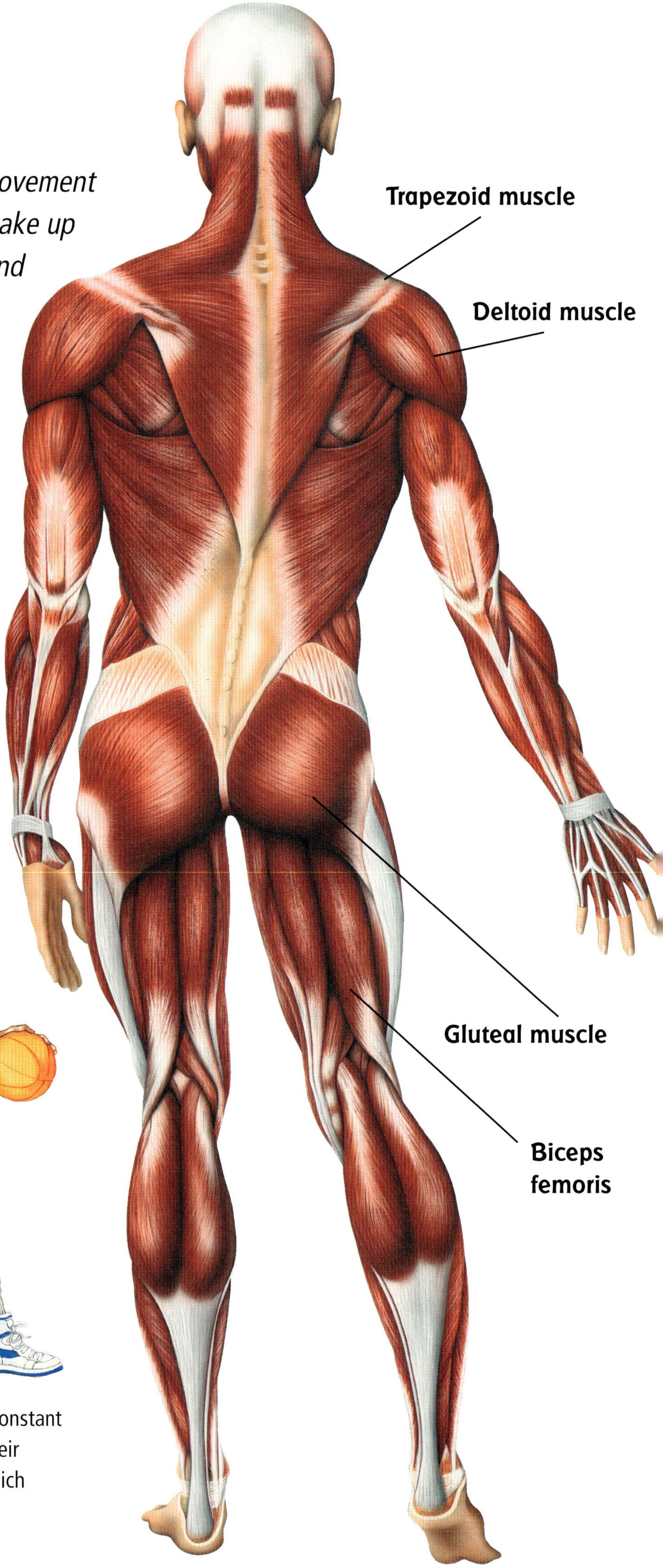

The skeletal muscles are joined to the bones by tendons. Tendons are made of collagen, a connective tissue which greatly strengthens them. Their weakest point is where they are attached to the bones, and this is where tearing may occur.

Athletes

Physical exercise improves muscle performance. With constant training, athletes are able to increase the volume of their muscle fibres and also the number of blood vessels which nourish them.

Fibres

Muscle fibres can produce energy slowly or rapidly. Slow fibre cells contain energy reserves, which means that they tire less quickly than fast fibres. Fast fibre cells contract very quickly but their energy reserves are soon depleted.

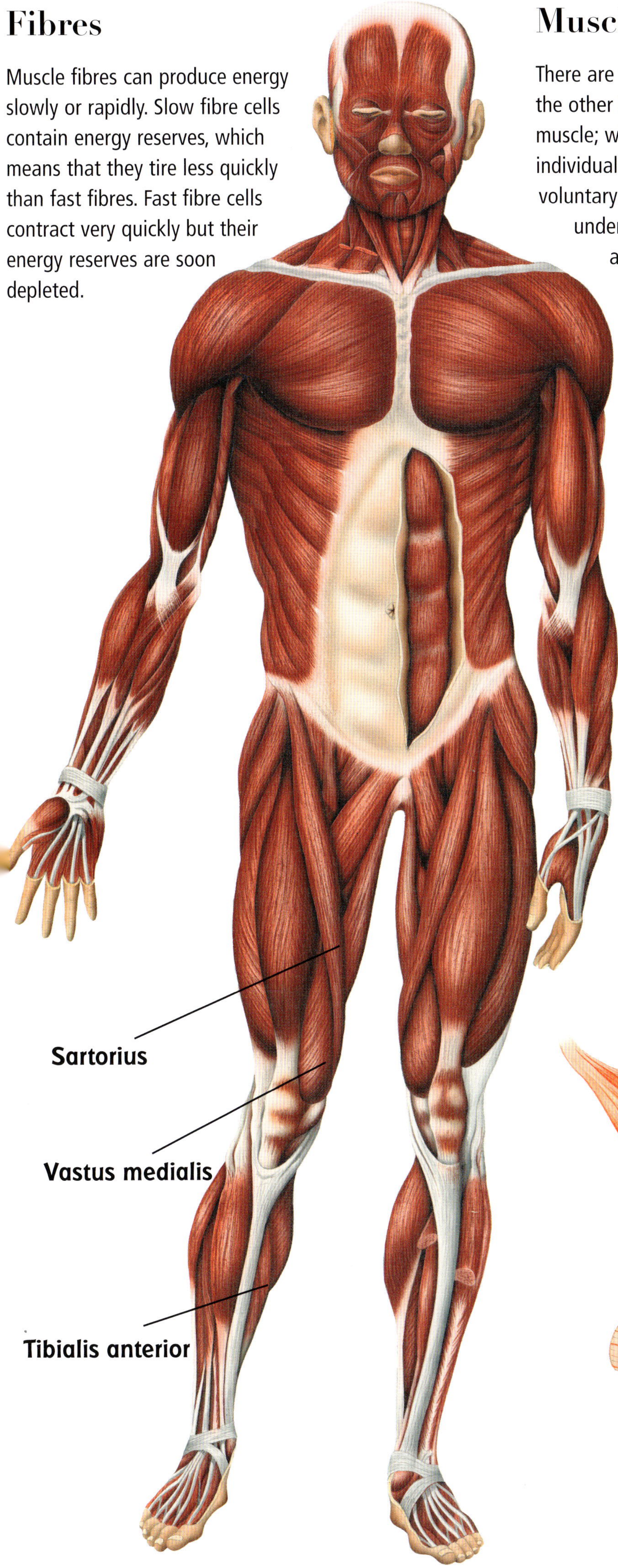

Muscle tissue

There are two different types of muscle tissue: one is striated and the other is smooth. Another specific tissue is that of the heart muscle; while it resembles striated muscle tissue, it has its own individual and unique characteristics. Striated tissue is found in the voluntary muscles, or those that perform intentional movements under the direct control of the brain (for example, the hand and foot muscles, or the eyelids).

Skeletal muscles all work voluntarily. Each one is composed of a variable number of slender bundles of muscle (fasiculi) covered with an external sheath. Inside each fasiculus are hundreds of muscle fibres containing myofibrils, made up of two types of protein called actin and myosin. These myofibrils pull together and cause the muscle to shorten or lengthen.

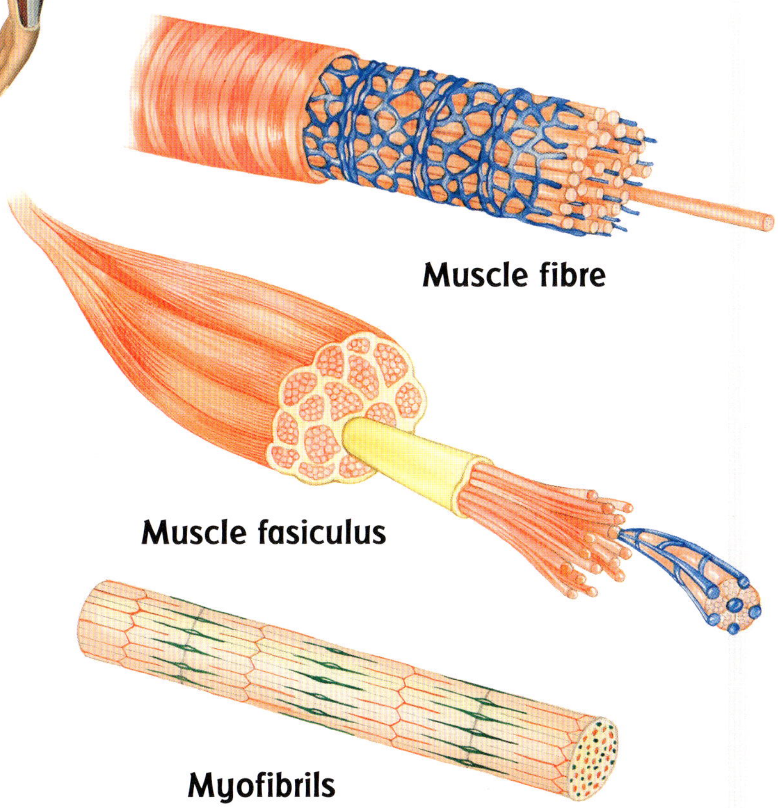

DIFFERENT MUSCLES

Muscles are formed from elasticised tissue that springs back to its original shape after contraction. This elastic action takes a very long time to complete. So that these movements will not be too slow, another muscle (an antagonist muscle) comes into play to accelerate this process.

Hand

The muscles of the hand are designed to allow a number of movements. The thumb is located opposite the other digits and is essential for picking up objects with strength and precision. The thumb and the little finger move via a series of muscles located in the hand itself, whereas the three central fingers are connected by long tendons to muscles in the forearm, which control finger movement. This system gives strength to our hand movements and enables us to carry out very fine work for long periods of time.

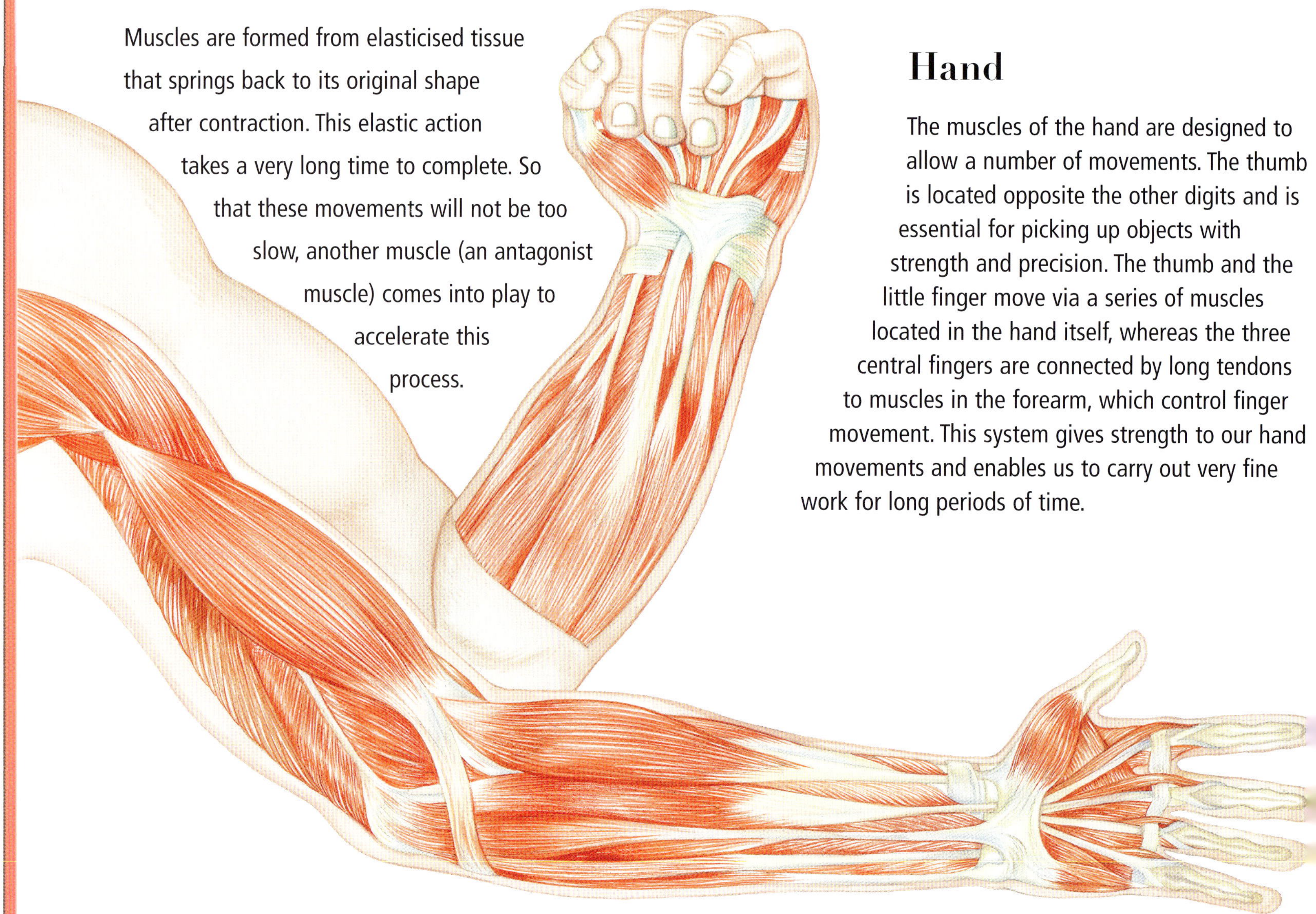

Antagonist muscles

The antagonist muscles can reach the bones connected to them due to the shortening effect of muscle contractions. Only the work of another muscle, acting in opposition to the first, can put the bones back into their original position. Two muscles working in opposition to each other are referred to as antagonists.

The triceps and biceps are a pair of antagonist muscles. When the biceps contract, the triceps relax, and vice versa. Their coordinated action allows the forearm to move.

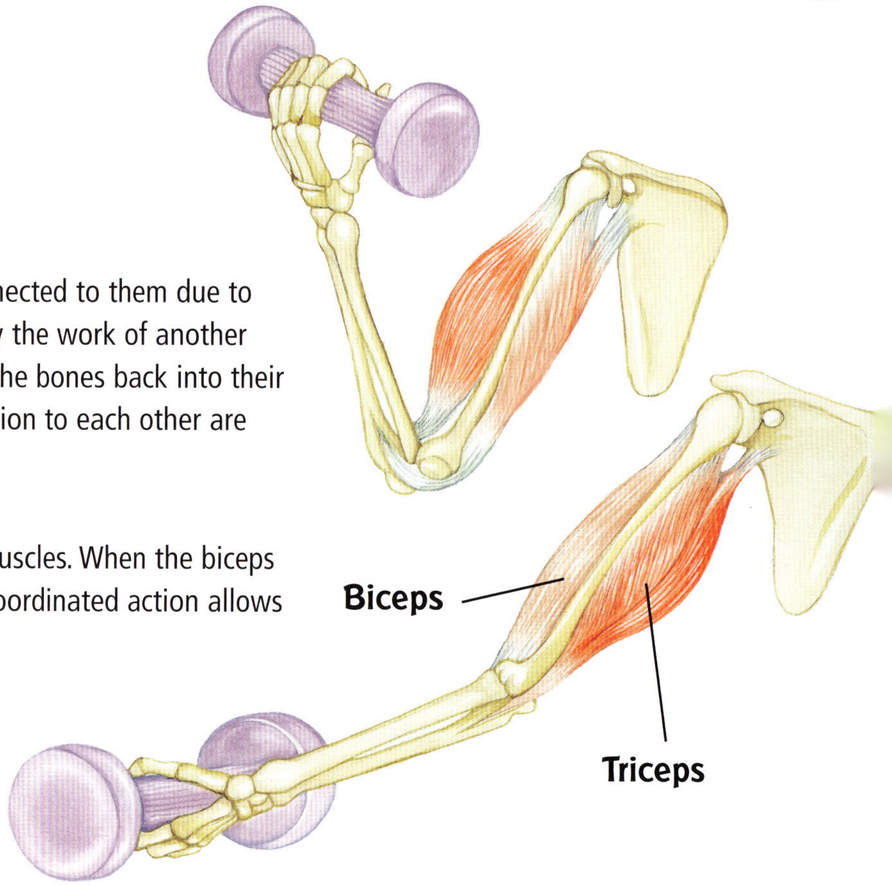

Sleepy facial expression

Surprised facial expression

Sad facial expression

The face muscles allow us to adopt a wide range of very different facial expressions. If we look in a mirror we can see the effects of about 30 different muscles at work. Both smiles and frowns are produced by relaxing or contracting all these muscle bundles.

The facial muscles are known as 'orofacial', because they cause the mouth and face muscles and the skin to move.

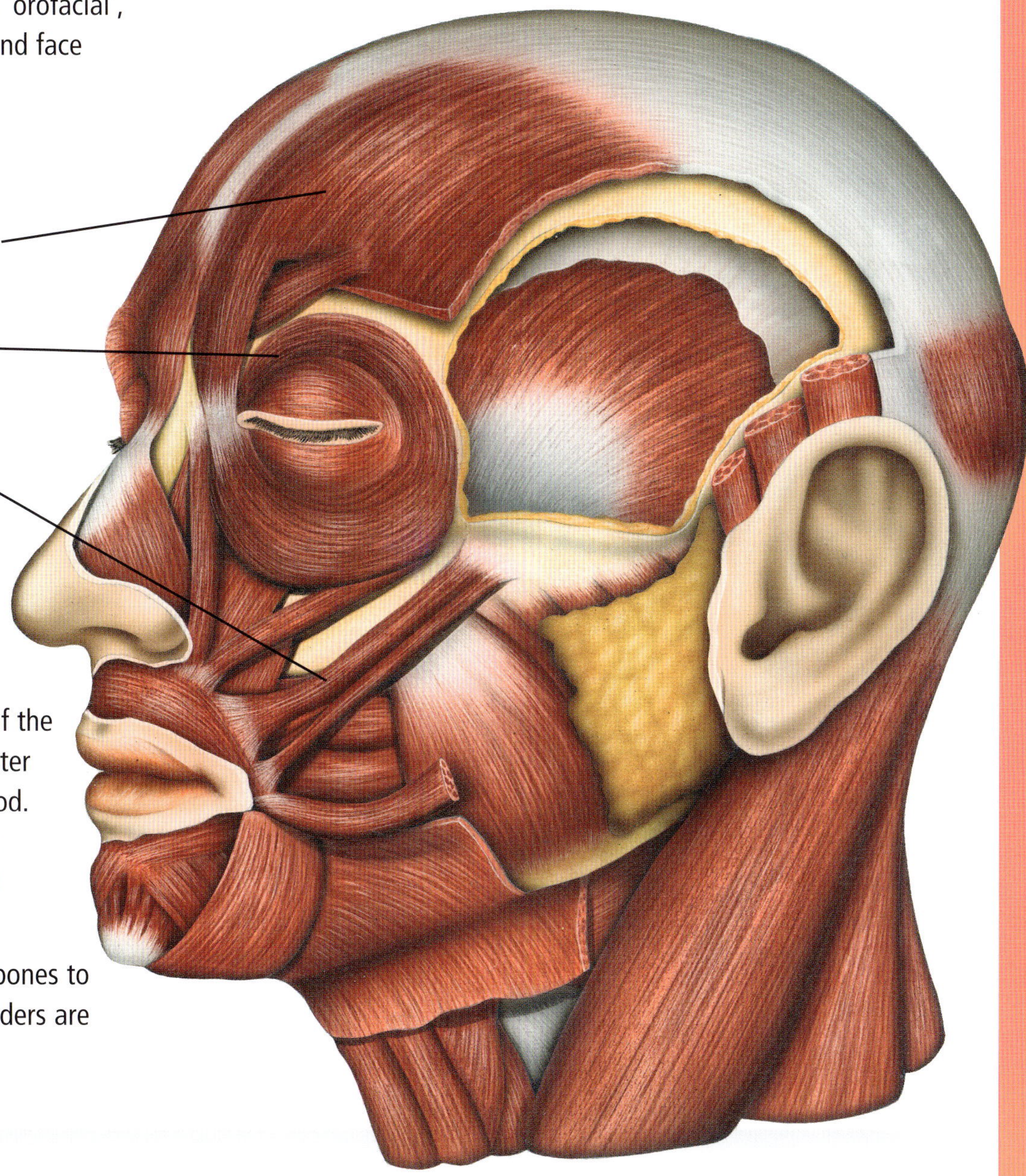

Muscles cause the eyelids to open and close in thousands of movements each day. Another of the most used muscles is the masseter which allows us to chew our food. While it is not a large muscle, it can exert a bite force of around 100 kilograms.

The muscles linking the cranial bones to the bones in the neck and shoulders are responsible for head mobility.

THE NERVOUS SYSTEM

The nervous system controls the activities of the human body, from the simplest of vital functions to the most complex of our thoughts. It is made up of two parts. The first is the central nervous system comprising the brain (encephalon), spinal cord, and the cranial and spinal nerves.

The second is the autonomous nervous system, divided into the sympathetic and parasympathetic systems. The whole of this dense network of nerve connections maintains contact between the brain and all the other parts of the body. Signals are transmitted by minute electrical currents generated by salts.

The basic unit of our whole nervous system is a cell with a unique shape, called a neuron.

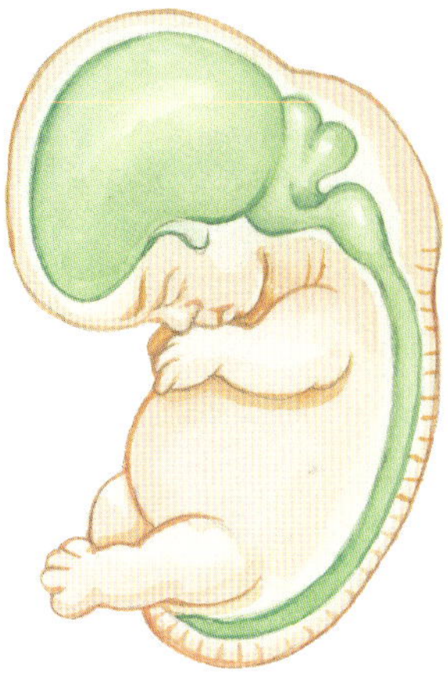

Neurons

Our lifetime supply of neurons is formed during pregnancy. The few nerve cells present in the embryo multiply with amazing speed. During this period before birth, the first connections between neurons are formed. This is also the time when axons develop and connect with different parts of the brain. After birth, the number of neurons slowly diminishes, a process which continues throughout our lifetime.

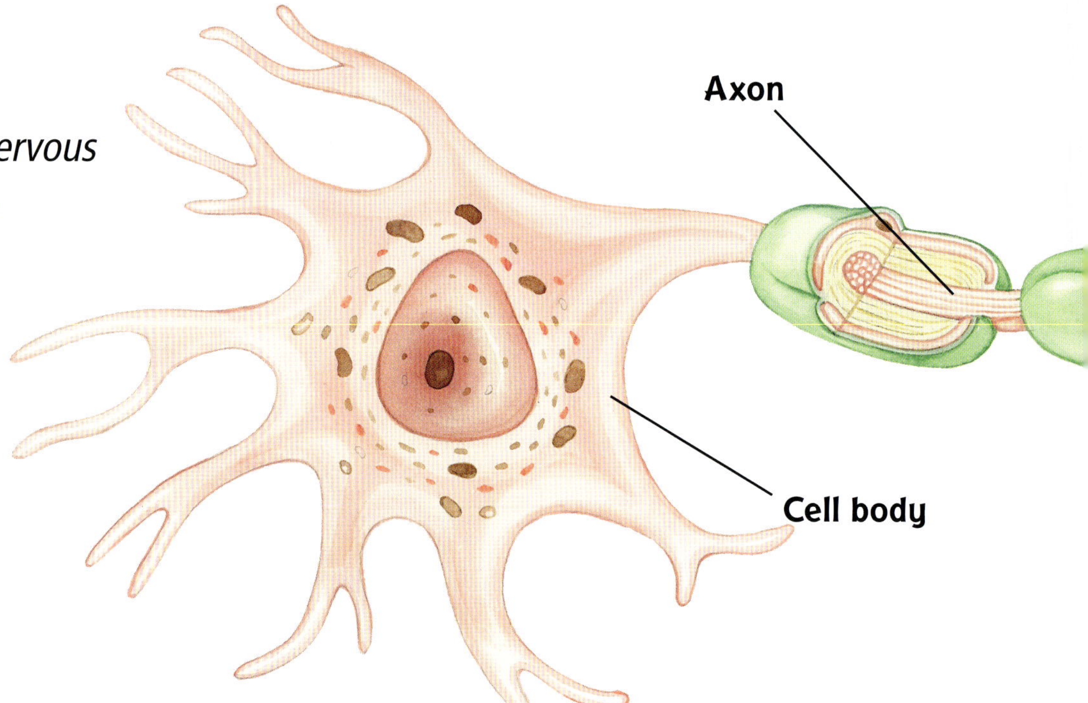

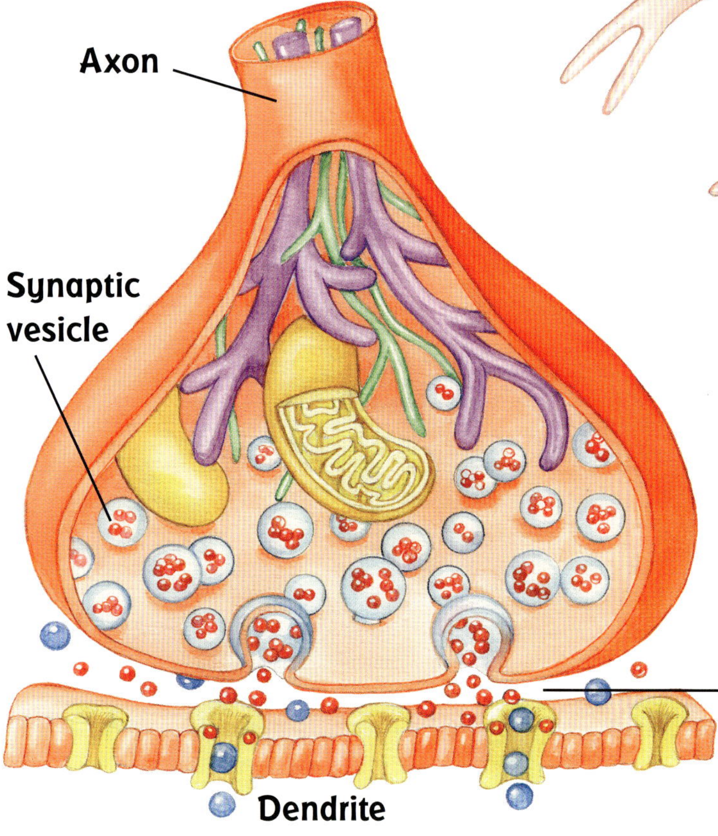

Synapses

These are the connections between nerve cells and join the axons in one neuron to the dendrites in another. Inside the synapses are small vesicles containing a chemical called a neurotransmitter. When the electrical impulse sent to the axon arrives at the synapse these vesicles release the neurotransmitter, creating a chemical bridge with the membrane of the neighbouring cell, and transmit the message.

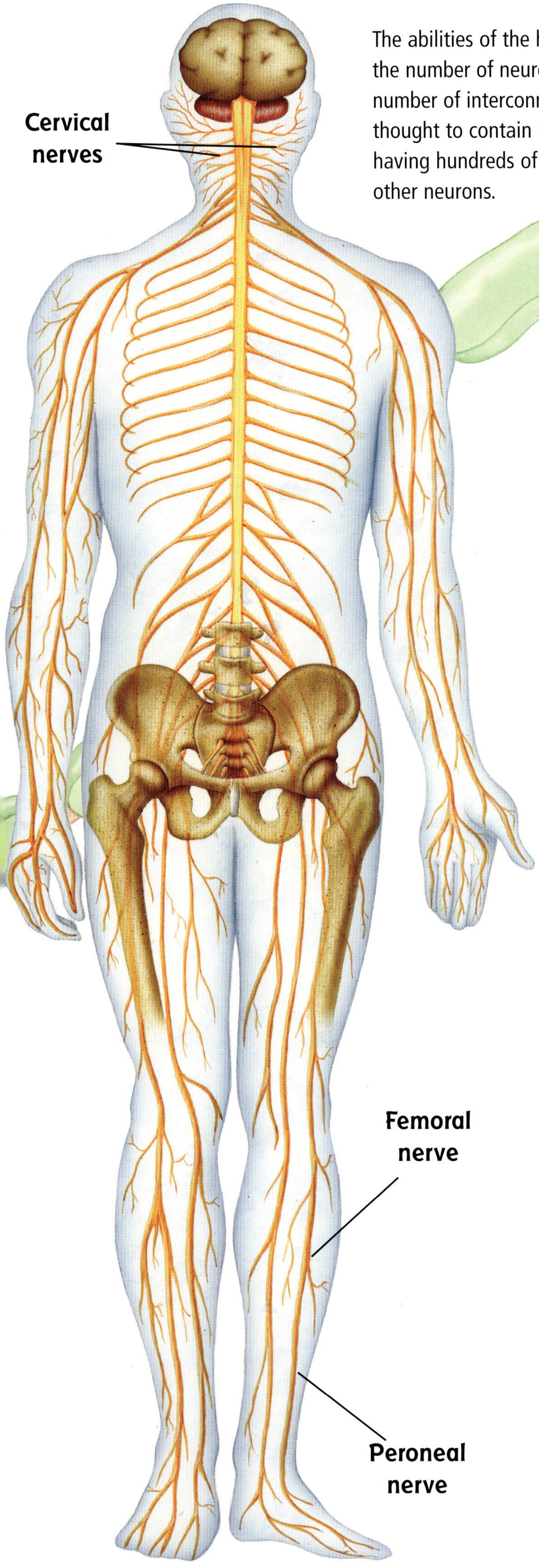

The abilities of the human brain mostly depend on the number of neurons it contains, and also on the number of interconnections linking them. The brain is thought to contain 100 billion neurons, each one having hundreds of connections to other neurons.

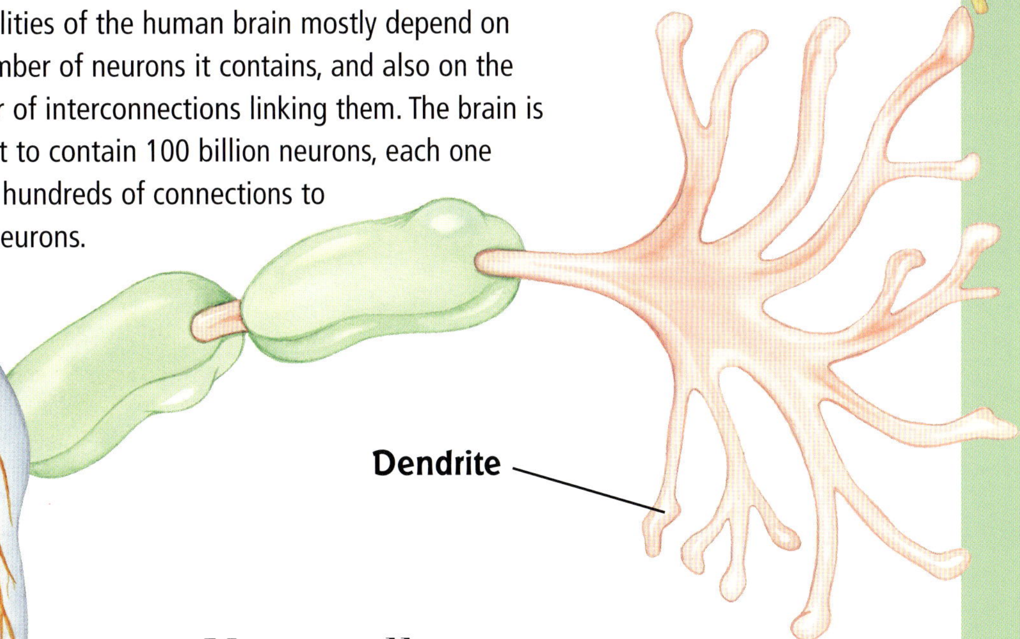

Nerve cells

Each neuron is a cell that can exchange information with other neurons. It is made up of a nucleus surrounded by a membrane to which dendrites and the axon are attached. The dendrites are branches that receive information from other neurons or from the external environment and send these messages to the nucleus of the neuron. The axon is the filament which sends electrical signals from the neuron to the brain. It may measure up to one metre in length. Often, it splits into several branches. At the top of the axon are tiny sacs known as synapses.

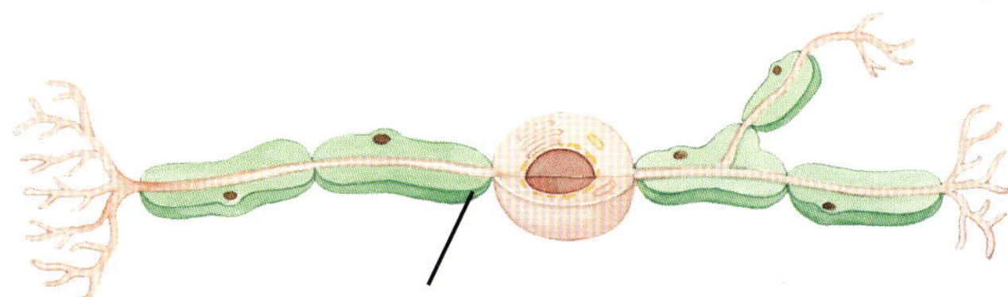

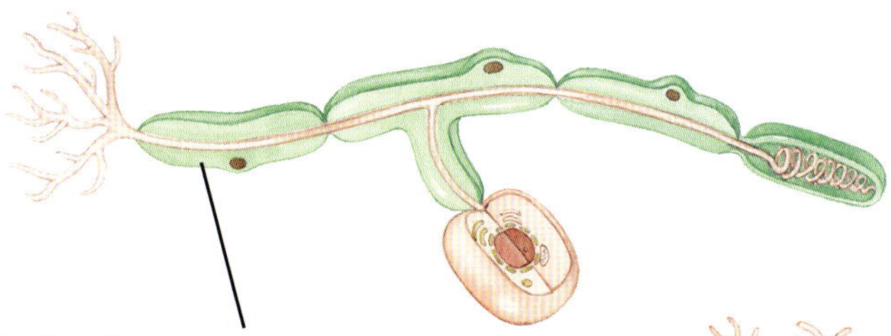

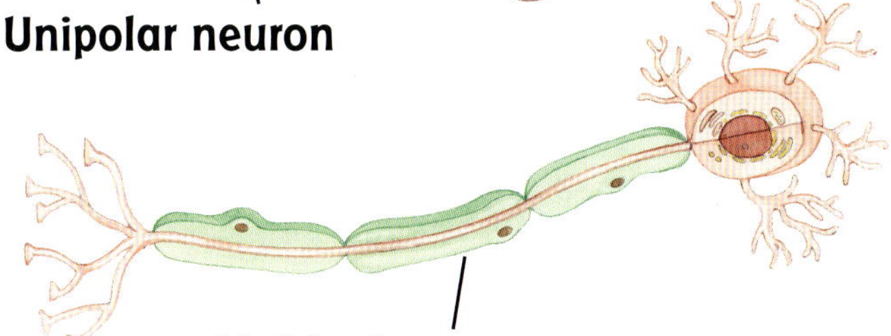

THE AUTONOMIC NERVOUS SYSTEM

Certain activities carried out by the human body are not directly controlled by the brain but are regulated by the autonomic nervous system. The muscles of the digestive, respiratory and urinary systems are coordinated by this autonomic system which also controls the heartbeat. In fact, within the autonomic nervous system are two sub-systems: the sympathetic and the parasympathetic. They fulfil opposite functions.

The role of the sympathetic system is to accelerate muscle activity, while the parasympathetic system slows it down. The combined effect of these two systems maintains the perfect balance for muscle activity. But sometimes one system may dominate the other. For example, in dangerous situations, our body speeds up its reaction time by the sympathetic system working overtime. During rest periods activity slows down, and this is when the parasympathetic system takes over.

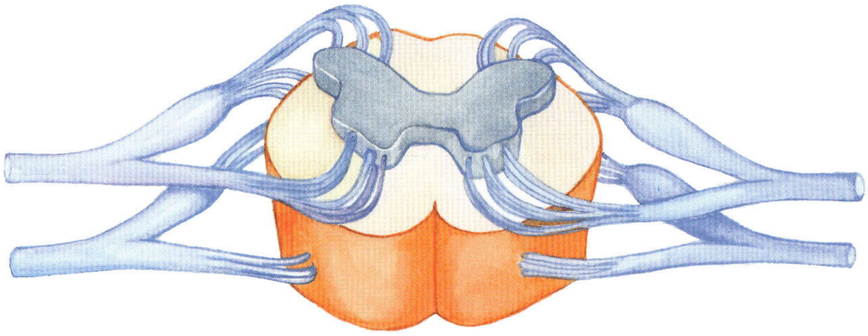

Spinal cord

Thirty-one pairs of nerves branch out from the spinal cord and travel out to every part of the body. The first eight pairs supply the neck area, 12 pairs serve the thoracic area, five pairs go to the lumbar region, another five pairs go to the sacral region, while the final one forms the coccygeal nerve.

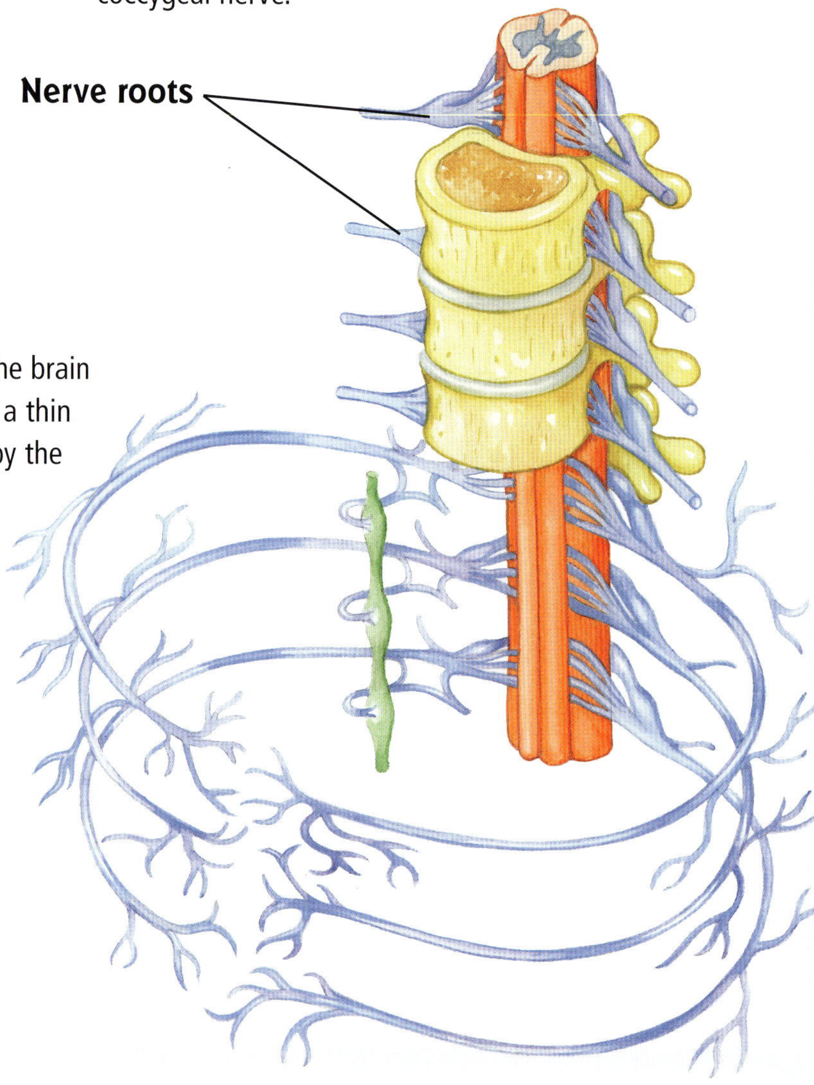

Spinal cord

The spinal cord consists of bundles of neurons linking the brain (encephalon) with the rest of the body. It is shaped like a thin cylindrical cord and runs down the bony canal formed by the vertebrae.

The delicate nerve structure of the spinal cord is covered with a bony shell which protects it from harm. The diagram represents a cross-sectional view of the central area occupied by the neurons, while connecting axons enter from the outside. Near each intervertebral space a pair of nerves branches out from the central cylinder. These nerves are known as sensory, motor or mixed.

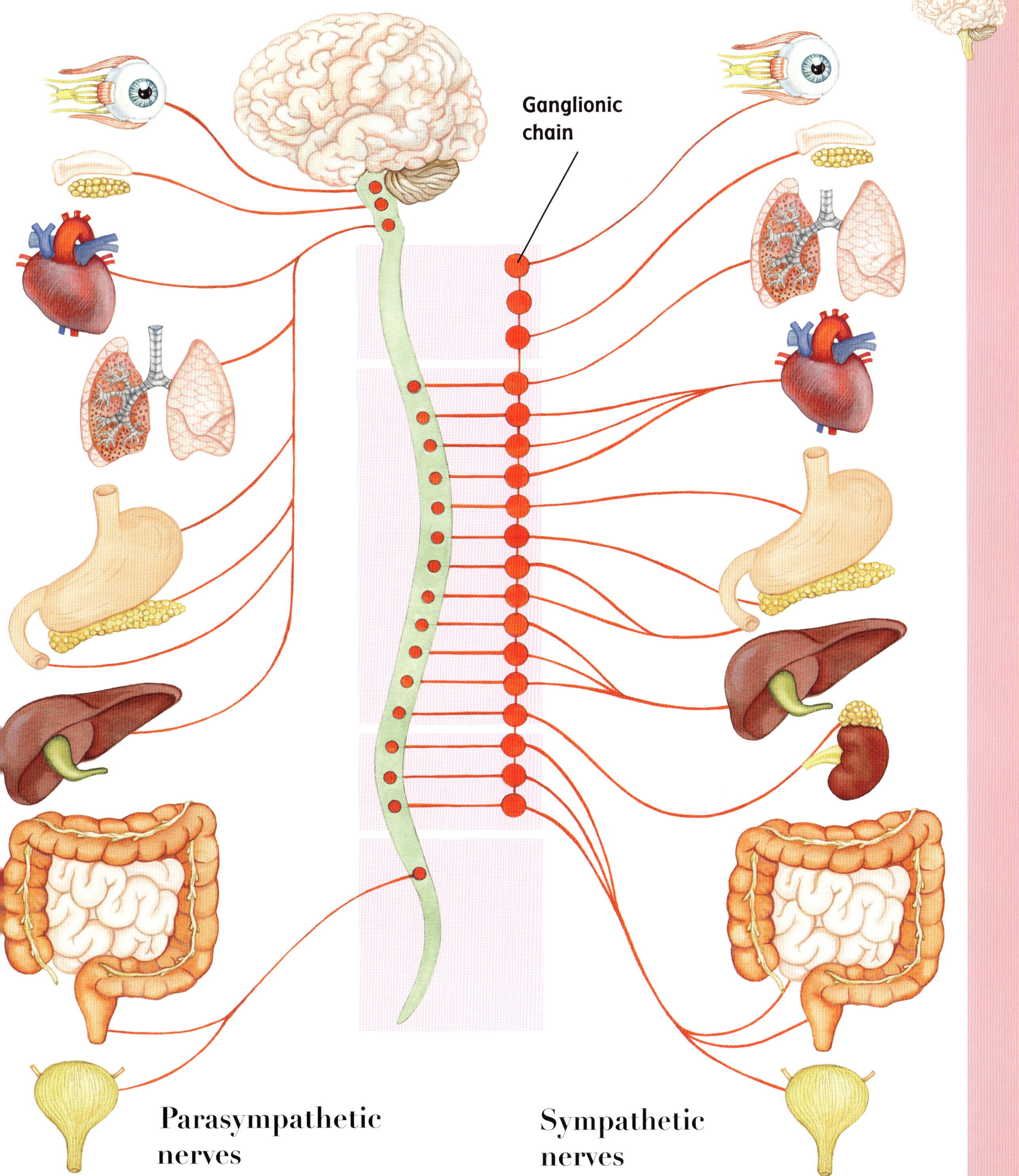

Parasympathetic nerves

Parasympathetic nerves stem almost exclusively from the base of the brain. This is exactly where the vagus nerve, the most important of the parasympathetic connections, begins. In the last portion of the spinal cord are the nerves which control the bladder and the lower segment of the intestine.

Sympathetic nerves

The sympathetic nerves leave the spinal cord but do not go directly to the muscles. Before reaching their destination, they cross a chain of ganglions (masses of nerve tissue) which coordinate their activity.

THE BRAIN

The most complex organ in the human body is the brain, or encephalon. It is enclosed in the skull, or cranium, and is composed of around 100 billion nerve cells called neurons. Its role consists of coordinating the vital activities of the body and formulating our thoughts.

The external part of the brain, the cerebral cortex, is quite thin, but it contains approximately 70 per cent of all our neurons. The cortex is divided into two hemispheres, separated by a deep furrow. Immediately below is the area where the two hemispheres connect, called the corpus callosum. Beneath the cortex is the limbic system. In this part of the brain our feelings develop. This is also where our memories are stored. In the deepest part of the brain are the thalamus and the hypothalamus. These regulate the hormones that control important functions such as sleep, hunger and aggression. At the rear of the brain is the cerebellum, which controls the muscles, ensuring that they move correctly and with precision. At the base of the brain is the brain stem linking the brain to the spinal cord.

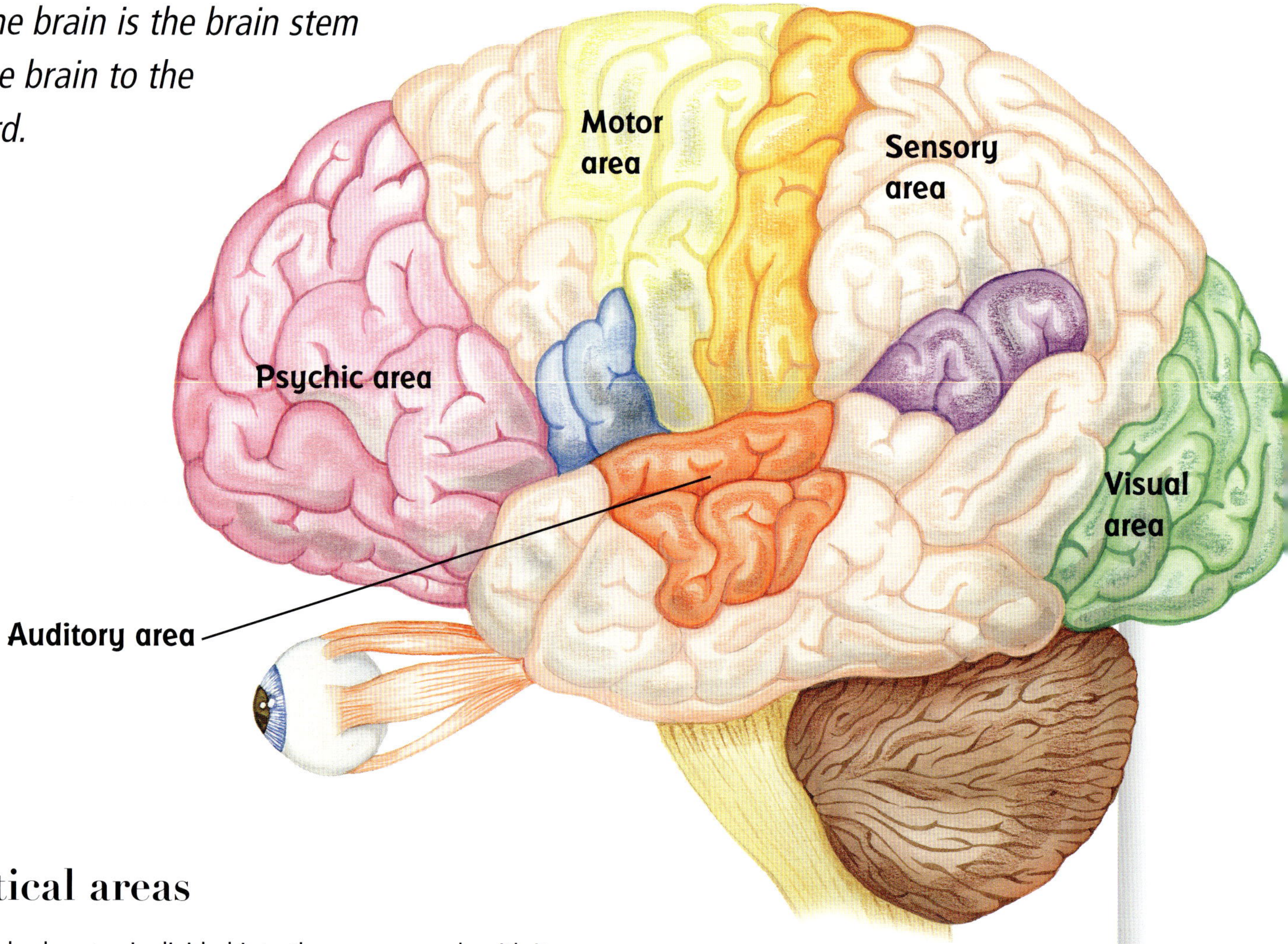

Cortical areas

The cerebral cortex is divided into three areas, each with its own particular functions. The sensory area receives stimulation from the sensory organs. The motor area sets the muscles to work, while the cognitive area coordinates the information received and matches it up with the information already stored in our memory. The coloured areas in the diagram show the relationship of the cerebral cortex to the various parts of the body.

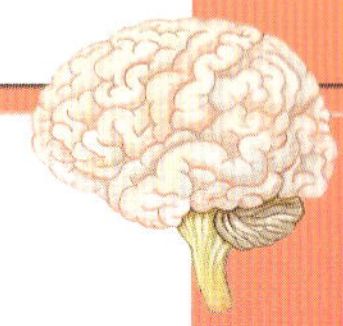

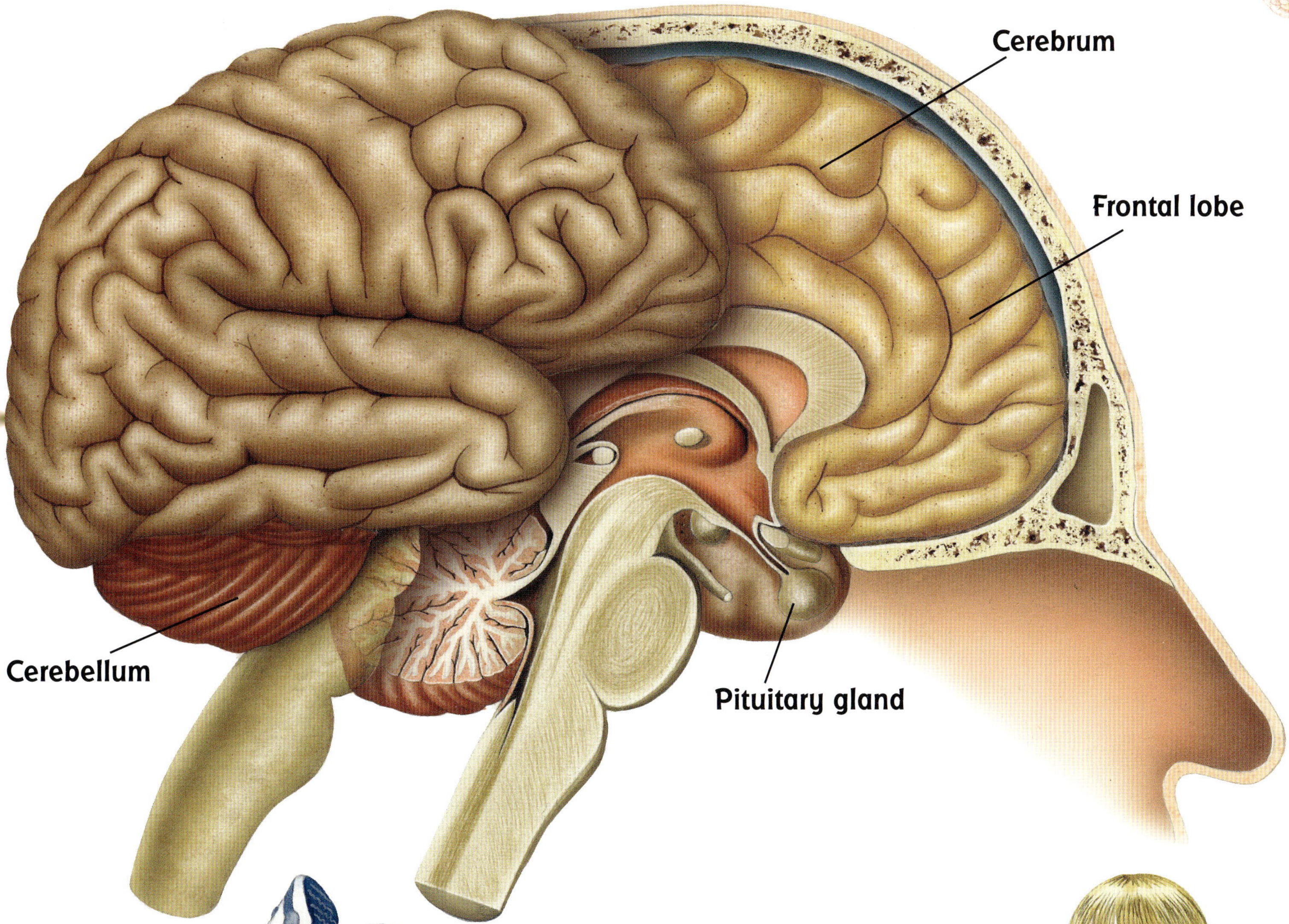

Whenever we feel that we have a particular gift for mathematics or that we are budding artists, we are simply drawing on a natural predisposition in our brain.

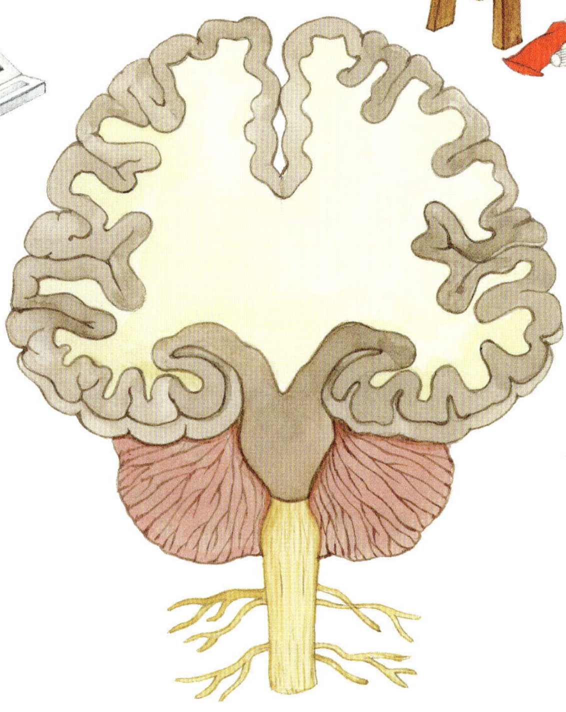

Left hemisphere

The two hemispheres are very different, and both are specialised in their own typical functions. The left side controls language, and steers us towards scientific activities.

Right hemisphere

The right side of the brain predisposes us to creative activities. This part of the cortex is the area which develops images and allows us to appreciate music.

THE EAR

The ear plays two important roles. Firstly, it captures soundwaves and transforms them into nerve stimuli, which it then sends to the brain. Secondly, it controls the body's sense of balance. This organ consists of three parts: the external ear, comprising the auricle and the auditory canal, which channels sounds to the eardrum (tympanum); the middle ear, comprising a series of small bones called ossicles, which transmit sound vibrations; and the internal ear, containing the cochlea, where the organ of Corti is located. Deep inside the inner ear are the three semicircular canals, which help us to maintain balance.

Organ of Corti

The organ of Corti transforms soundwaves into nerve impulses which are then sent to the brain. It contains sensitive cells with fine hairs, which are able to pick up vibrations in the fluid moving about inside the cochlea.

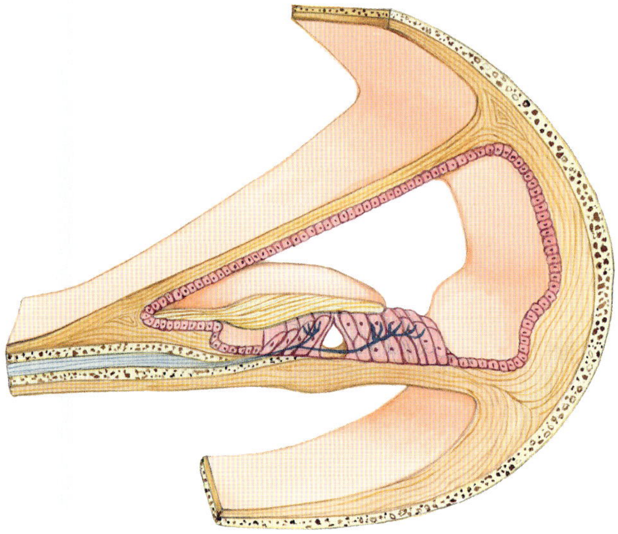

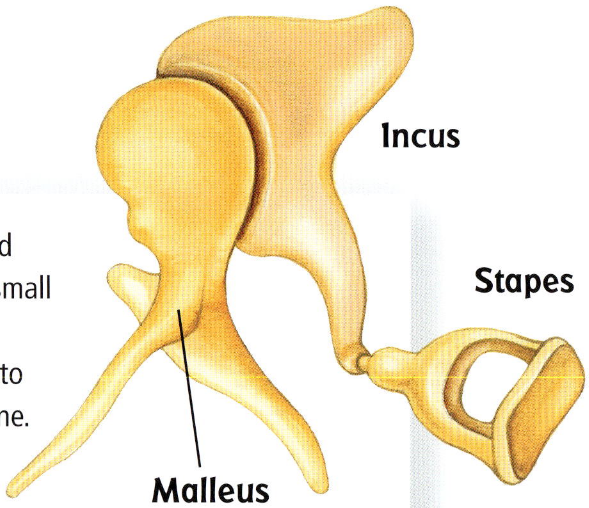

The malleus, incus and stapes are the three small bones (ossicles) that connect the eardrum to the cochlear membrane. They are able to amplify the force of sound vibrations up to twenty fold.

Cochlea

The cochlea is a spiral-shaped organ about three centimetres long. The interior is hollow and divided into three channels. The ascending and descending ramps (scala tympani and scala vestibuli) are connected at their ends by a small hole known as the helicotrema. Inside is the perilymph, a transparent fluid that vibrates due to movement of the stapes, a small stirrup-shaped bone that presses against the membrane known as the fenestra of the vestibule. Vibrations of the perilymph are transmitted to the fluid in the central channel via contact with the organ of Corti.

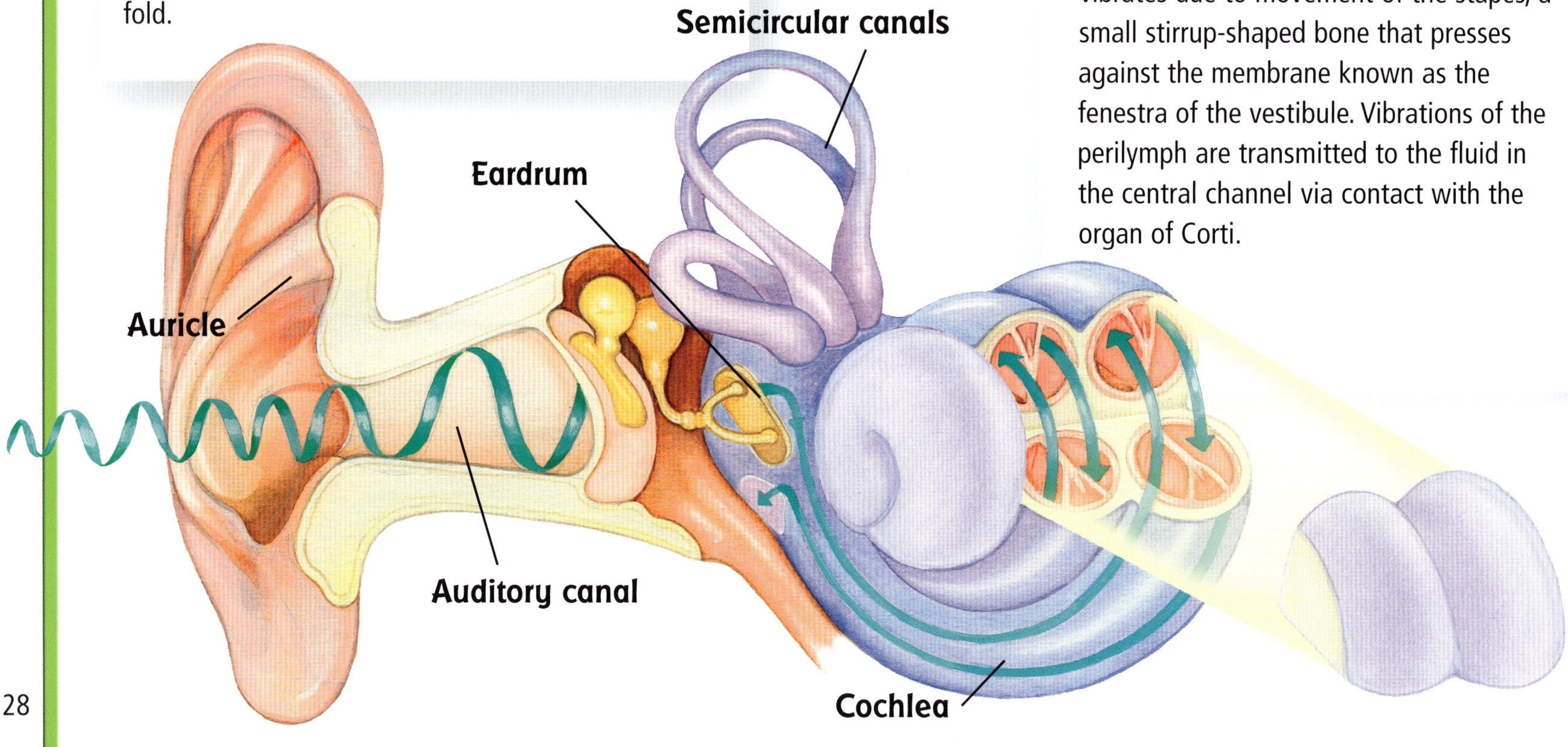

Eustachian tube

The inner ear is connected to the nose and pharynx by the Eustachian tube. This opening allows the pressure to be equalised on both sides of the eardrum (tympanum). A rapid increase in height in an elevator can sometimes cause a difference in pressure and make the ears 'pop' or feel blocked. Swallowing saliva will usually correct this discomfort.

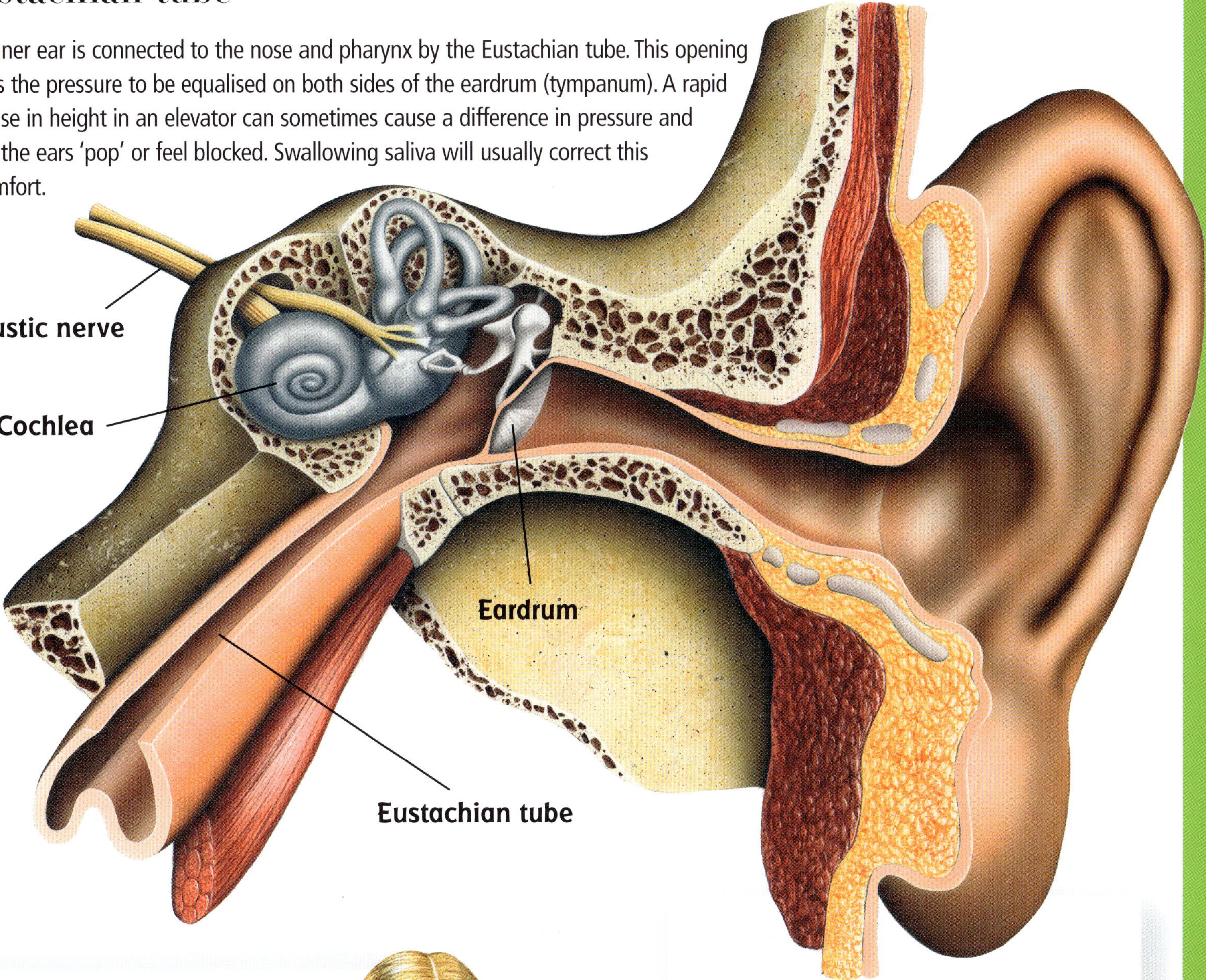

Our ears are able to recognise the direction of sound, provided it is heard more distinctly by one ear. To maintain this sensitivity, we must be careful not to expose our ears to very loud noise, which could be harmful.

Semicircular canals

The three semicircular canals are very important organs. They are located on three different levels and send information to the brain about the position of the body. At the end of each canal is an ampulla containing the sensory cells that record changes in the position of the body and the head.

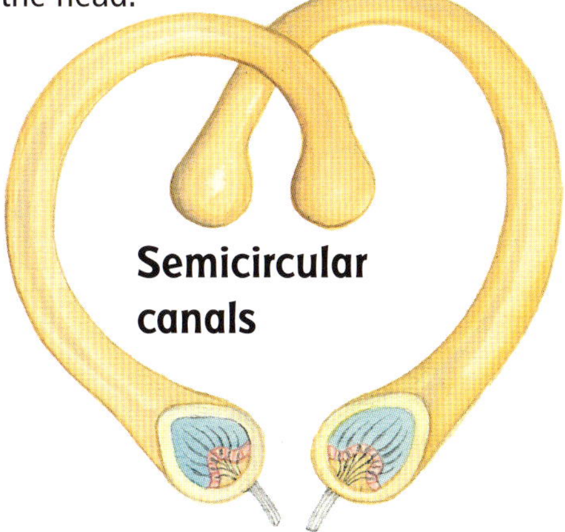

SIGHT AND THE EYE

The eye is the visual organ. It is round in shape and contains a transparent jelly-like substance called the vitreous humour. The sclera is the thick, opaque external coating of the eyeball. The anterior part or cornea is transparent. The intermediary choroid membrane contains a dense network of blood vessels. In conjunction with the cornea, the choroid forms the iris, a group of muscles that control light passing through to the retina. The iris is rich in pigments, which serve to protect the eye from excessive light. The quantity of pigment varies from one individual to another and determines eye colour.

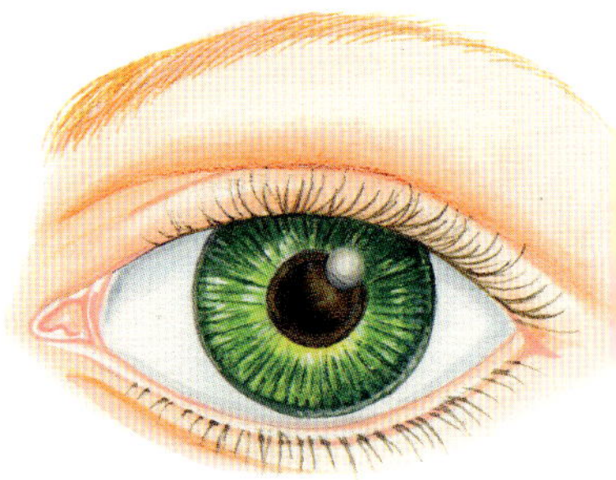

Green iris

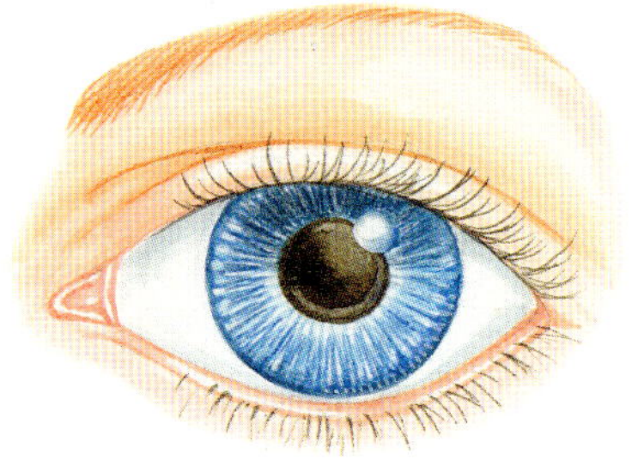

Blue iris

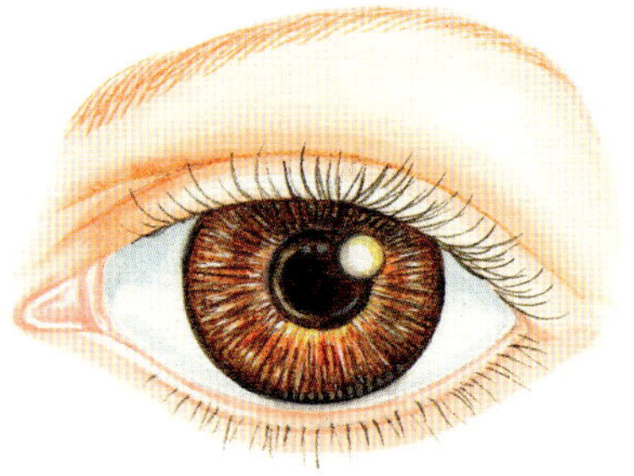

Brown iris

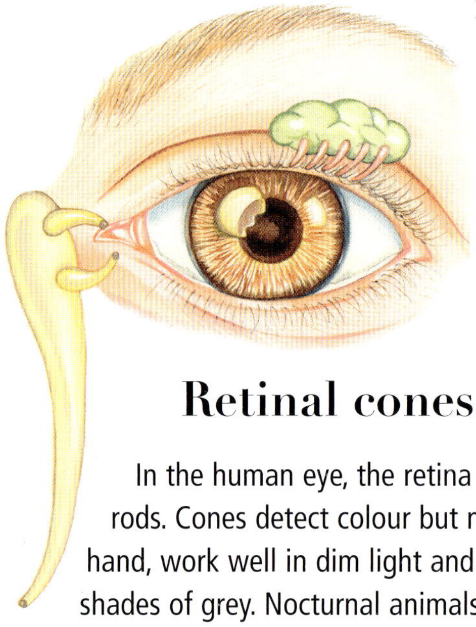

Retinal cones and rods

In the human eye, the retina contains two types of light-sensitive cells: cones and rods. Cones detect colour but need bright light to work well. Rods, on the other hand, work well in dim light and allow us to distinguish different shades of grey. Nocturnal animals have large numbers of rods, which allow them to see in the dark. But since they do not have cones, they are unable to distinguish different colours.

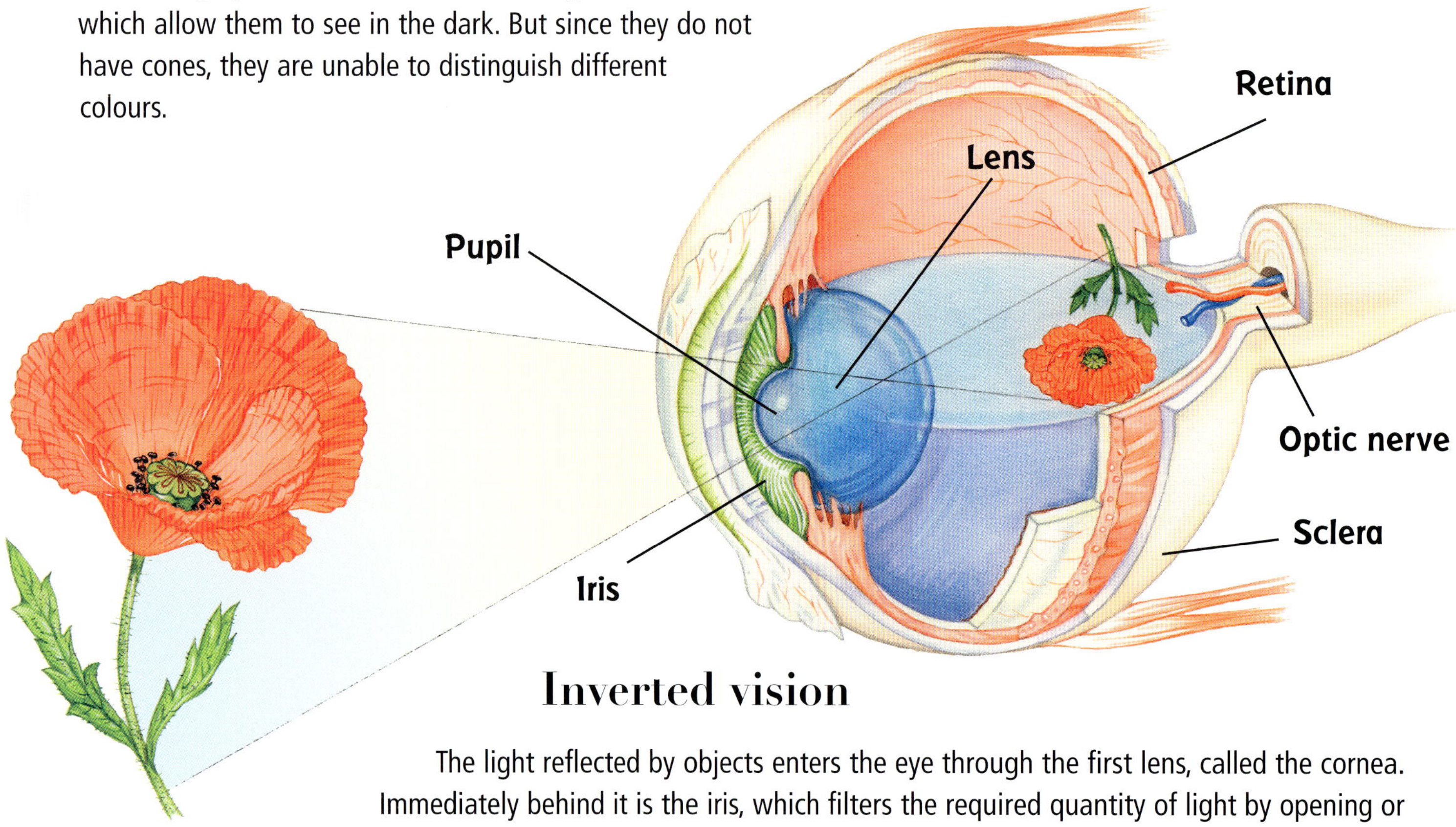

Inverted vision

The light reflected by objects enters the eye through the first lens, called the cornea. Immediately behind it is the iris, which filters the required quantity of light by opening or closing the hole in the centre, called the pupil. Behind the pupil is the double crystalline lens, which can focus light on the retina. This system of lenses creates an inverted image on the back of the eye, which is then turned the right way up by the brain.

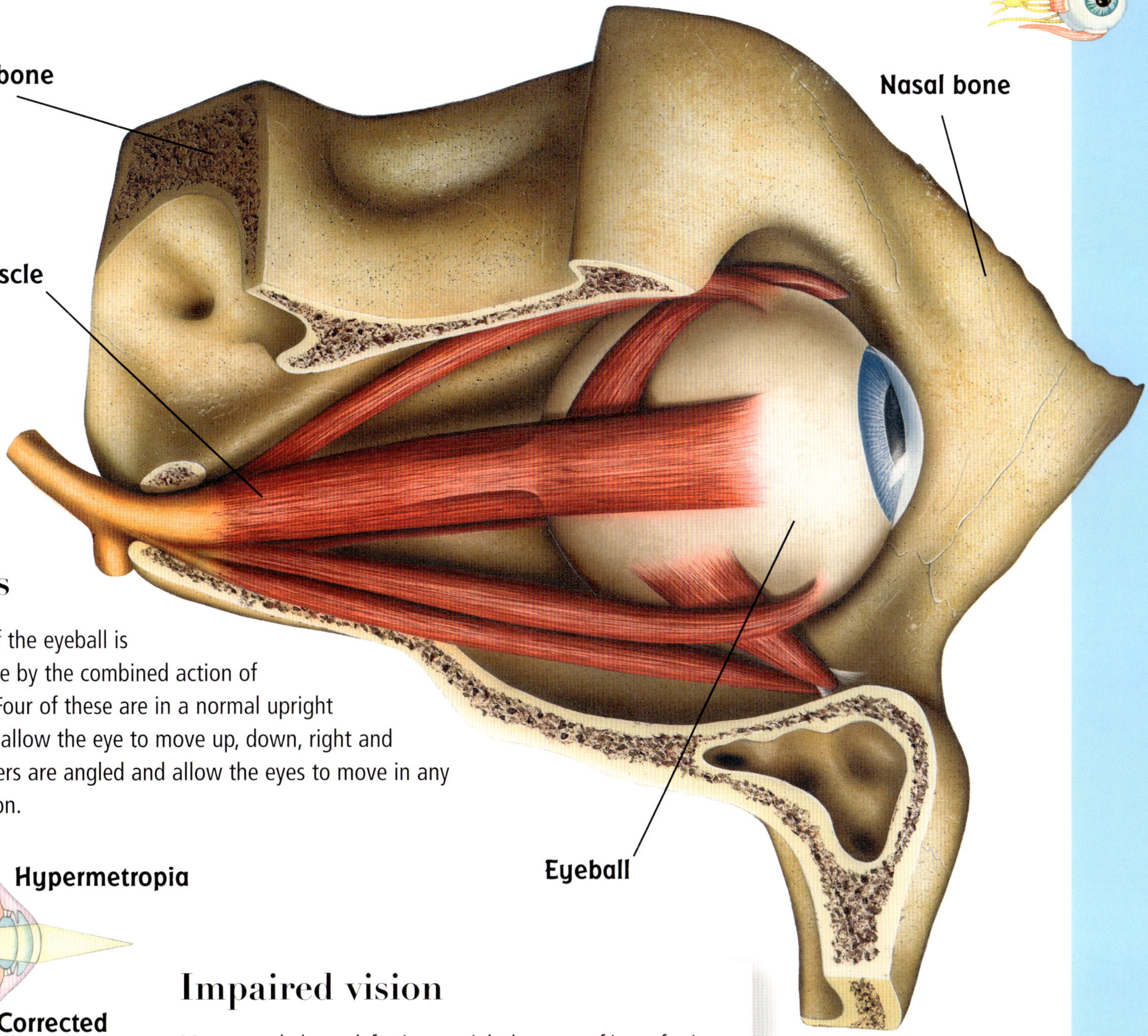

Muscles

Movement of the eyeball is made possible by the combined action of six muscles. Four of these are in a normal upright position and allow the eye to move up, down, right and left. Two others are angled and allow the eyes to move in any other direction.

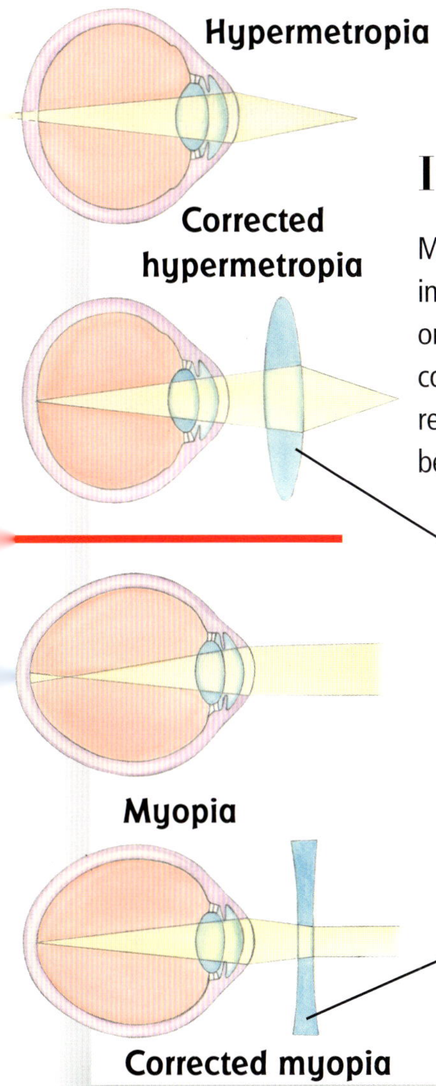

Impaired vision

Many people have defective eyesight because of imperfections in the system which conveys images. If the eyeball is too long or too short, or if the crystalline lens is not functioning correctly, the image cannot focus correctly on the retina. Fortunately, most of such defects can easily be corrected by the use of glasses or contact lenses.

SMELL AND TASTE

The olfactory (smelling) organ is located inside the nose. The two nasal cavities have external openings called nostrils, and internally these are connected to the upper part of the pharynx. The posterior part of the nasal cavity is lined with respiratory mucosa, which becomes the olfactory mucosa in the upper section of the canal. The air we inhale through the nose carries odour molecules, which are conveyed to the olfactory receptors. It is not clearly understood exactly how the nose can distinguish so many different smells. Most probably, the various receptors are all different, with each one being sensitive to particular odour molecules. The combined stimulation of several groups of different cells allows us to distinguish about 1,000 smells.

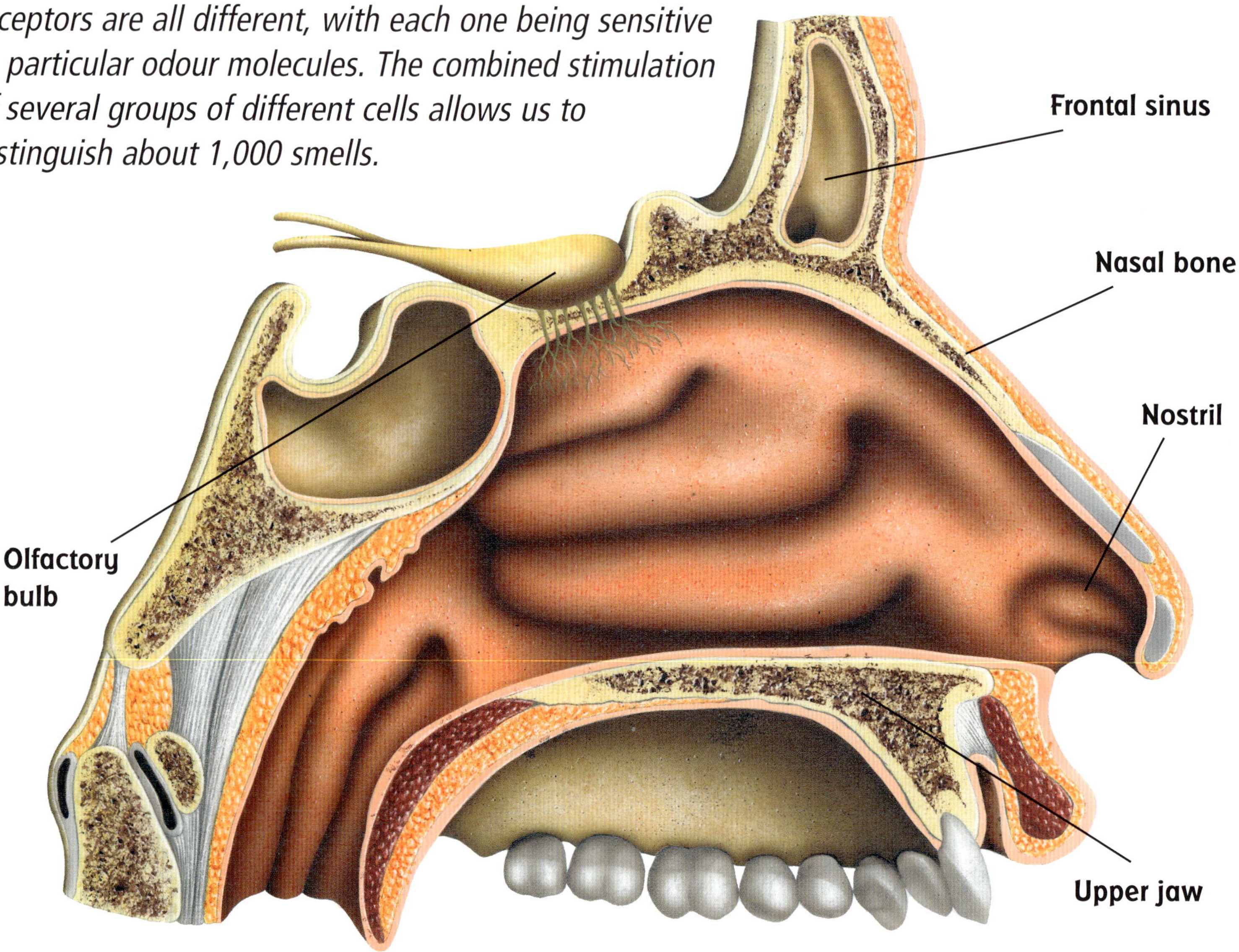

The olfactory mucosa

The smell receptors, or olfactory cells, have an elongated shape with a bulb in the centre that contains the nucleus. One of the two extremities has a tuft of tiny hairs, which are the real olfactory receptors. The other end is very long and thin, and forms part of the olfactory nerve fibres. These cells cover only a small area of the nasal cavity, which limits our ability to detect odours. Nevertheless, we can smell odours even when they are present in minute quantities.

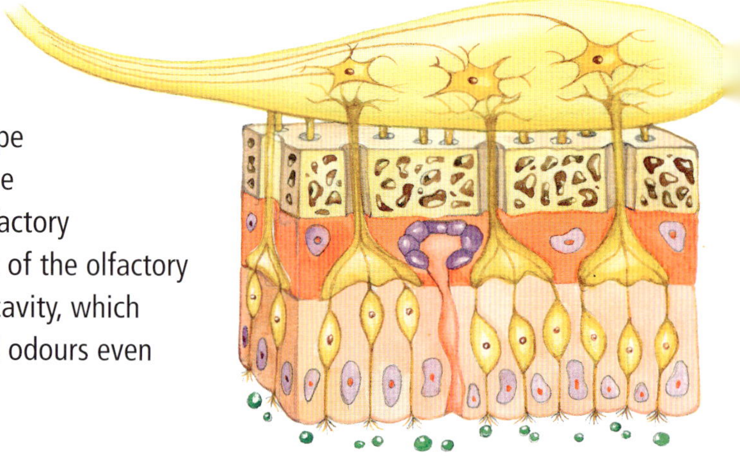

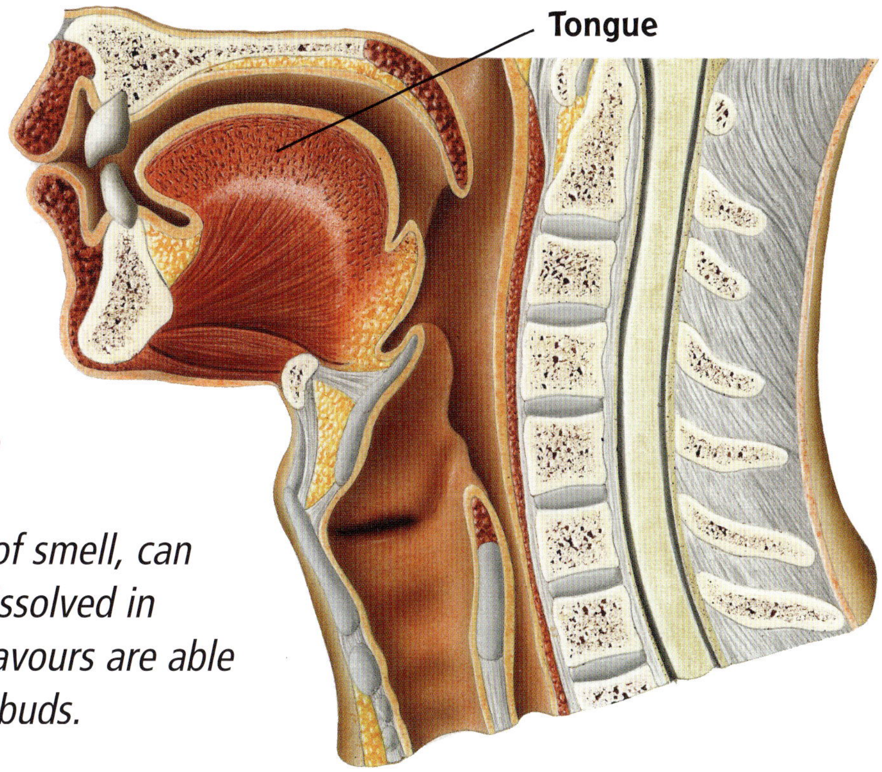

The tastebuds are located on the surface of the tongue. In children, the whole of the tongue surface is covered by them, whereas in adults only the tastebuds along the edges of the tongue are sensitive. We are able to recognise tastes because the tastebuds, assisted by our sense of smell, can discern the taste of substances dissolved in fluids; this is the only way that flavours are able to come in contact with the tastebuds.

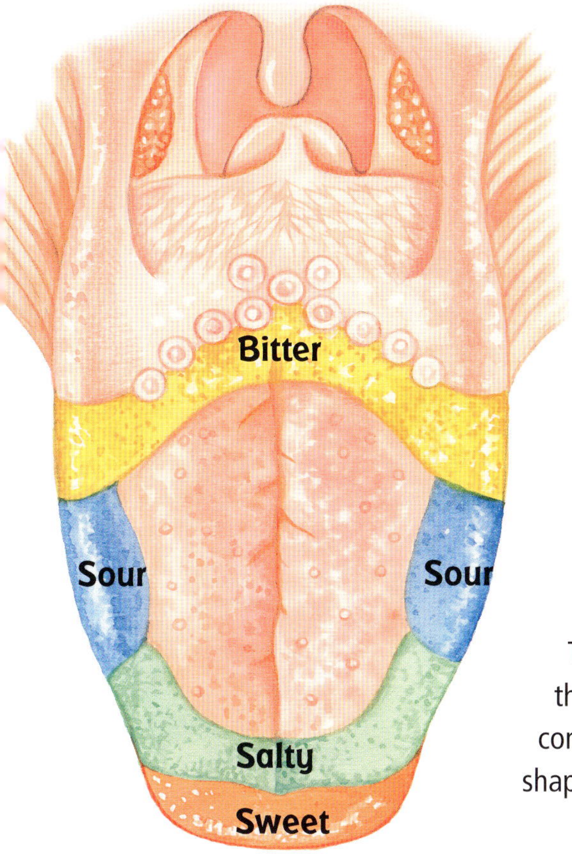

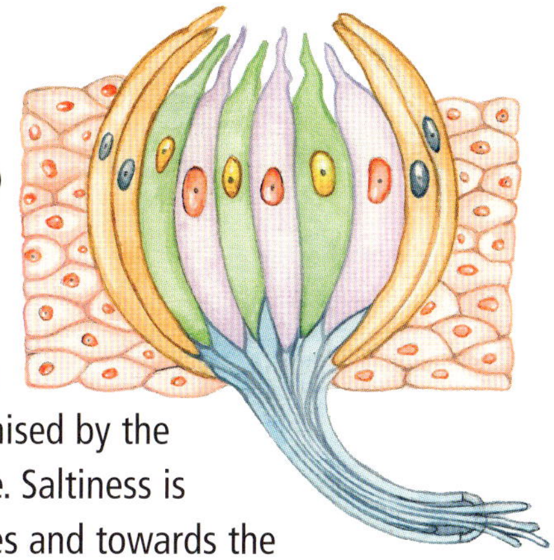

Sweet or sour

The tastebuds are able to distinguish four main tastes. Sweetness is recognised by the buds located on the tip of the tongue. Saltiness is identified by the buds along the edges and towards the front of the tongue. The buds on the sides of the back of the tongue are sensitive to sour tastes, while bitter flavours are picked up by the buds along the back part of the tongue.

Tastebuds

Tastebuds assume various shapes. On the point of the tongue are many long, thin and narrow filiform buds, which have tactile functions. The taste cells are contained in the mushroom-shaped fungiform buds. The largest are the cup-shaped calyces, which have on their surface tastebuds rich in nerve endings.

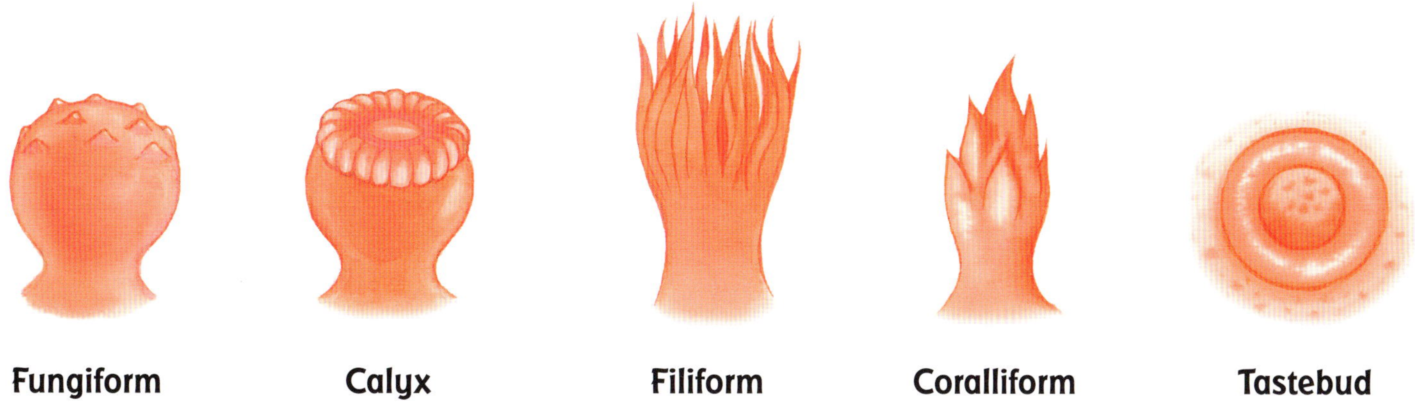

TOUCH AND SKIN

The human body is completely enveloped by skin, which offers insulation and protection from the environment. The epidermis, or the outermost part, is made up of several superimposed layers of specialised cells. The next layer, rich in melanocytes, produces the pigment melanin. Deeper down, the basal cells are able to create new cells to replace the dead ones. The intermediary tissue is known as the dermis. This contains a dense network of blood vessels, sweat glands, touch and pain receptors and hair follicles. The internal part is the hypodermis. Because this is composed of fat, it has excellent insulation properties.

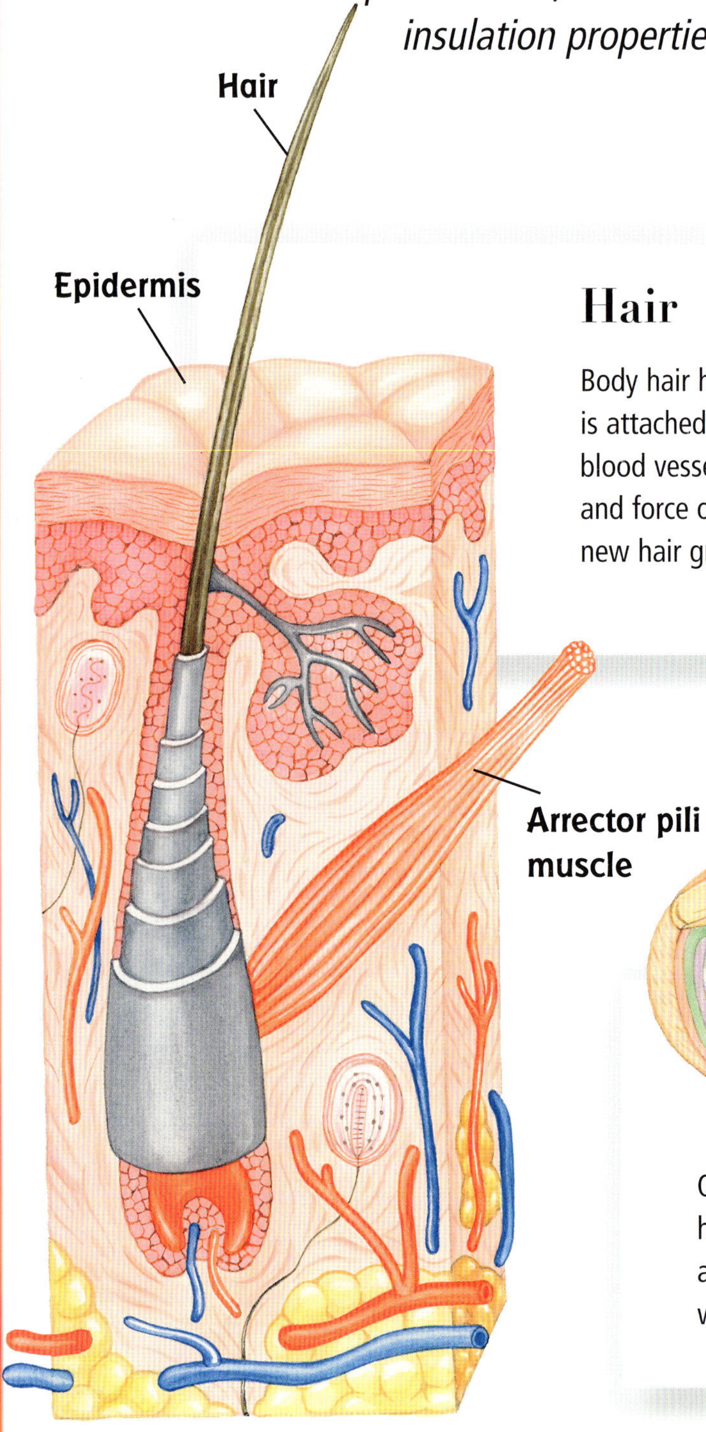

Hair

Body hair helps to keep the body warm. Each hair root is attached in the dermis and nourished by a tiny blood vessel. As new hair cells form, they grow upwards and force out the older ones, coming to the surface as new hair growth.

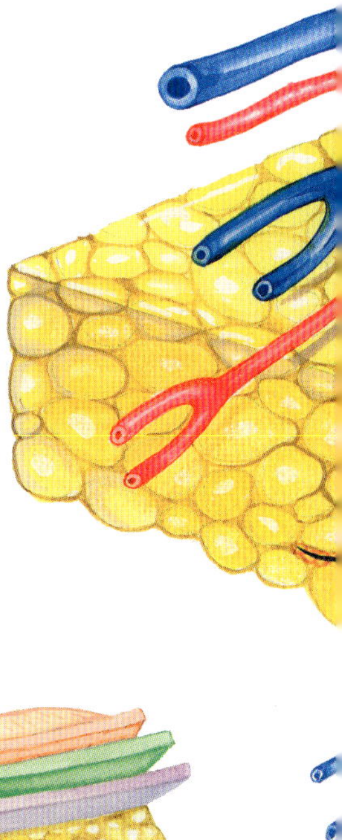

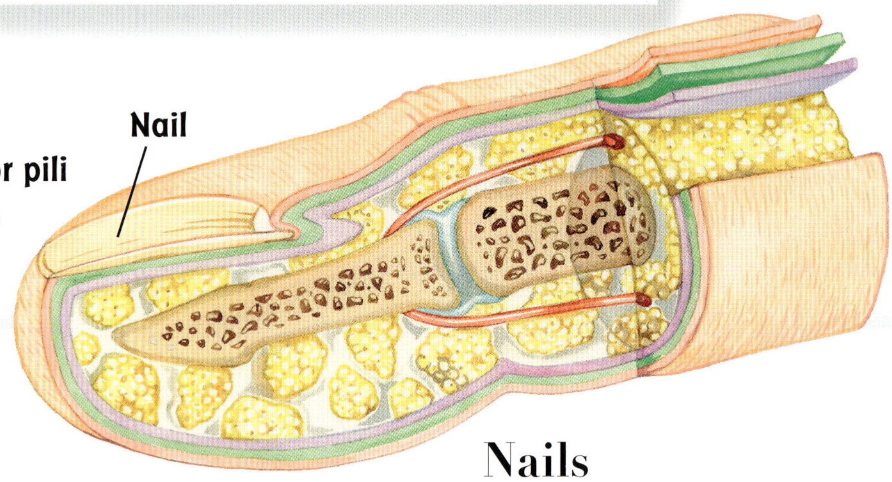

Nails

Our fingers and toes are protected by nails. They are made of a thin horn-like substance, and yet they have a certain sensitivity to touch. They are made from keratin, the same protein as the skin and are enriched with mineral salts.

Skin colour

Melanin is a dark pigment that produces skin colour. It helps protect the skin from the sun's harmful ultraviolet rays. Populations living in the sunniest geographic zones have larger quantities of melanin cells than those living in less sunny areas, so their skin is darker.

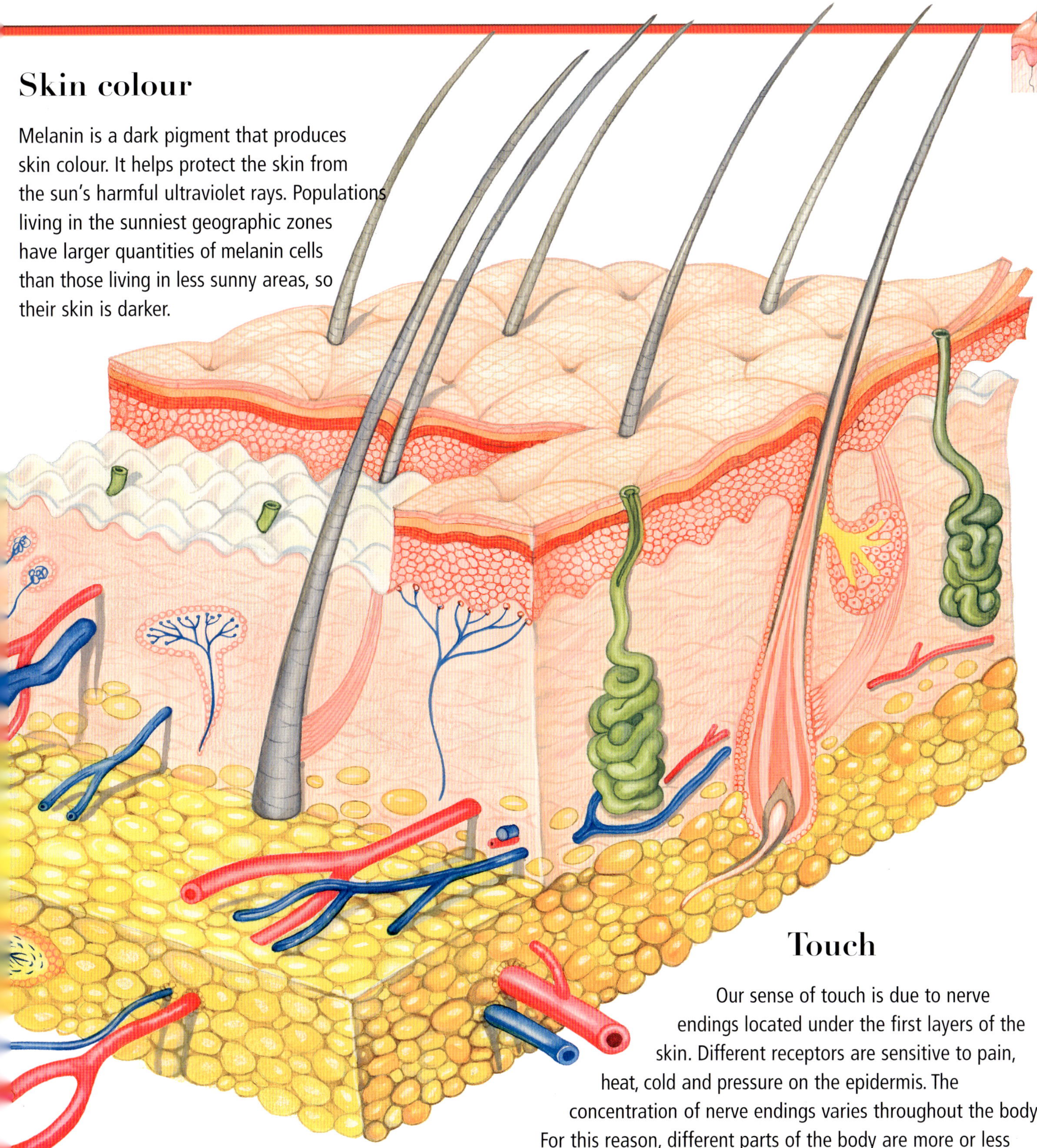

Touch

Our sense of touch is due to nerve endings located under the first layers of the skin. Different receptors are sensitive to pain, heat, cold and pressure on the epidermis. The concentration of nerve endings varies throughout the body. For this reason, different parts of the body are more or less receptive to tactile stimulation.

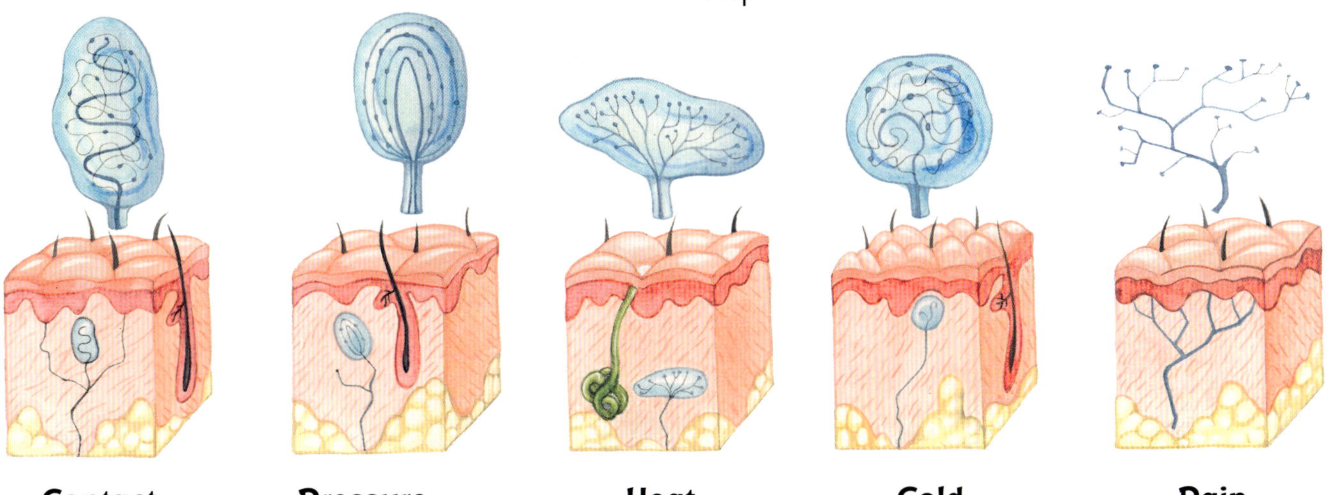

THE HEART

The heart is the muscular pump that keeps blood flowing around the body. This organ is located between the two lungs and is about the size of a clenched fist. It is composed of special muscle cells which have the ability to contract. The cells are grouped into fibres which perform the rhythmic movements required to produce a pumping action.

The heart is divided into four chambers: two atria and two ventricles. The atria receive blood from the veins and send it into the ventricles. Supplied with blood from the atria, the ventricles contract and force the blood into the arteries. The blood must always flow in the right direction. For this reason, there are two small atrio-ventricular valves located between the atria and the ventricles. Between the ventricles and the arteries are two half-moon-shaped, or semi lunar, valves. The right atrium and the right ventricle located beneath it work on blood that contains small amounts of oxygen, received via the veins, and send it to the lungs. The left atrium and left ventricle receive freshly oxygenated blood from the lungs, which is pumped through the whole body.

Phase 1: isometric diastole

The atria receive the blood and are filled, while the ventricles are mostly empty and relaxed.

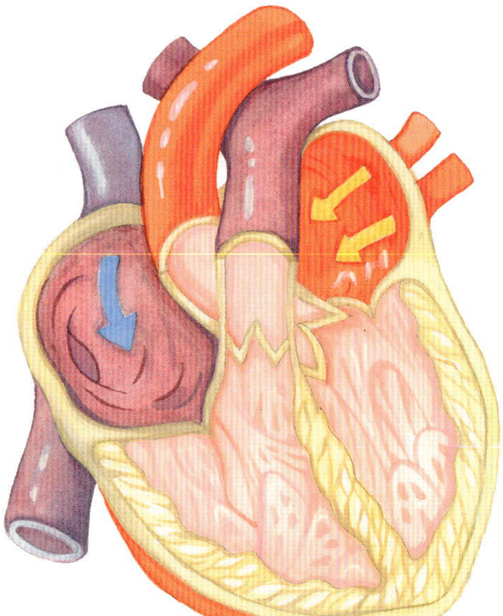

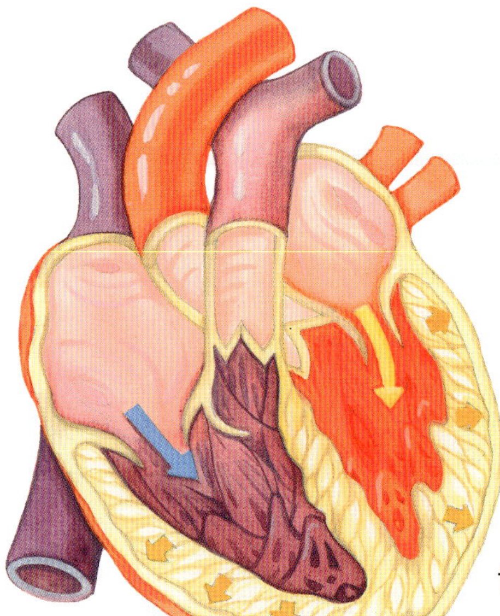

Phase 2: isotonic diastole

Pressure in the atria is strong, causing the atrio-ventricular valves to open. Blood flows into the relaxed ventricles.

Phase 3: isometric systole

The filled ventricles begin to contract. The atrio-ventricular valves close.

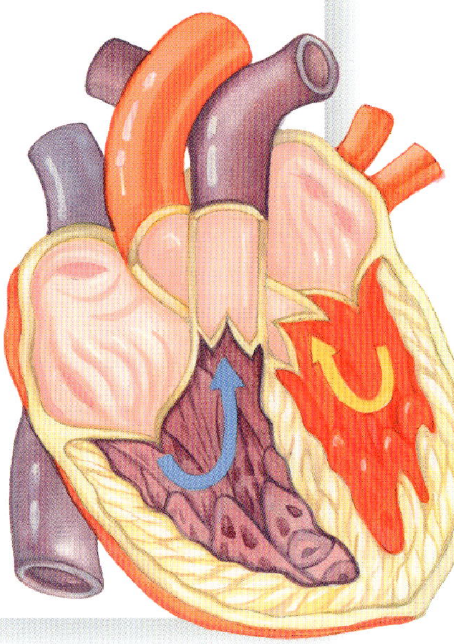

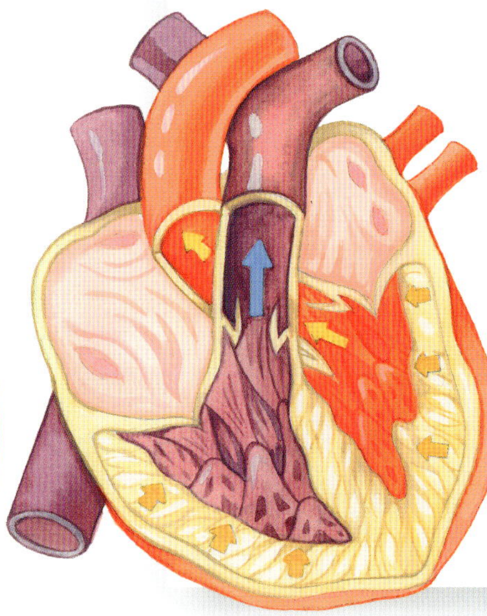

Phase 4: isotonic systole

Ventricular pressure is maximal. The semi lunar valves open, and the blood flows into the arteries.

Heart murmurs

When it is functioning normally, the heart produces a characteristic sound coinciding with a heartbeat. This is caused by the closing of the two atrio-ventricular valves, followed after a brief interval by the semi lunar valves. If valve performance is not normal, blood reflux will occur. This produces a particular sound known as a murmur, indicating that a cardiac valve is not functioning correctly.

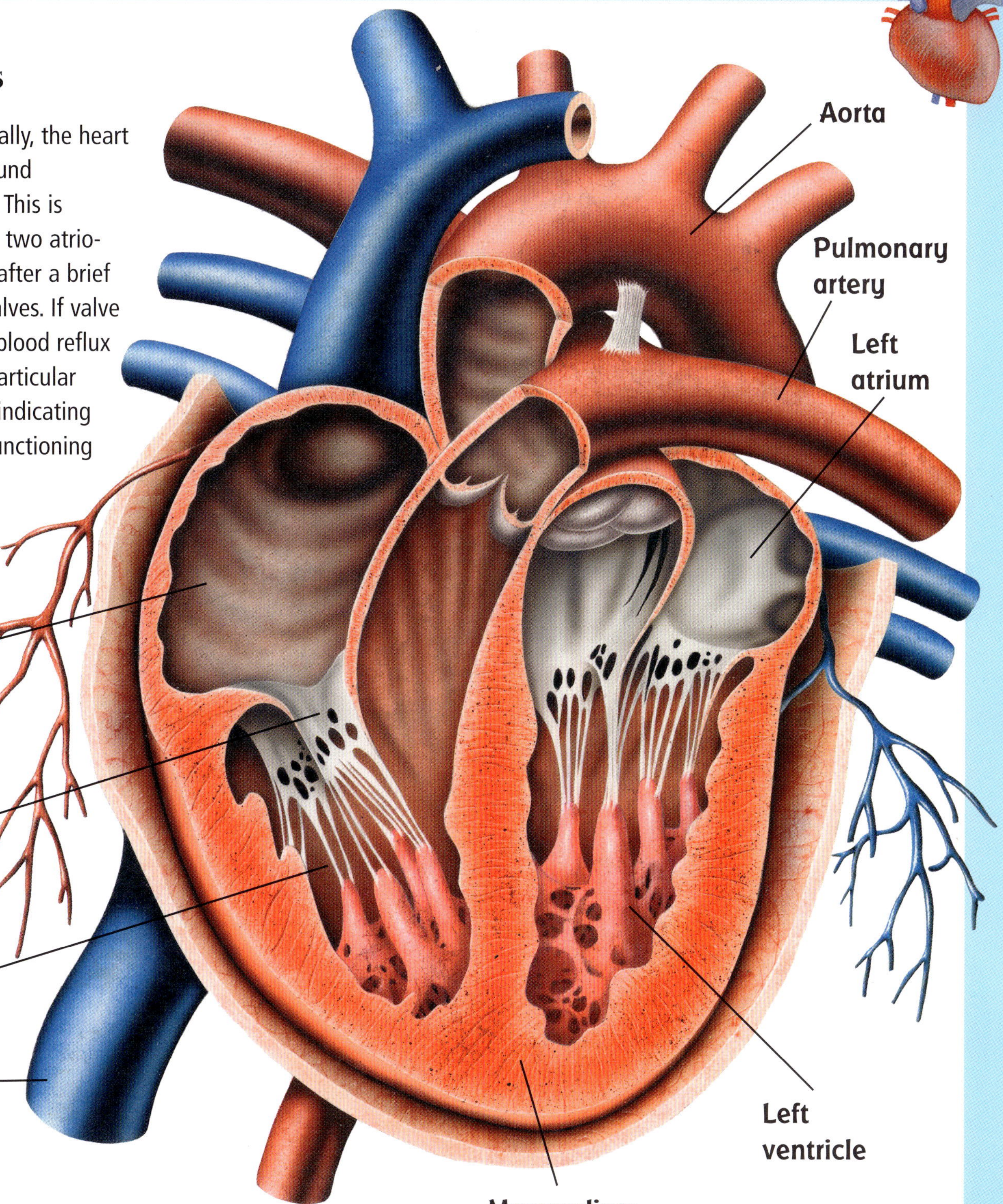

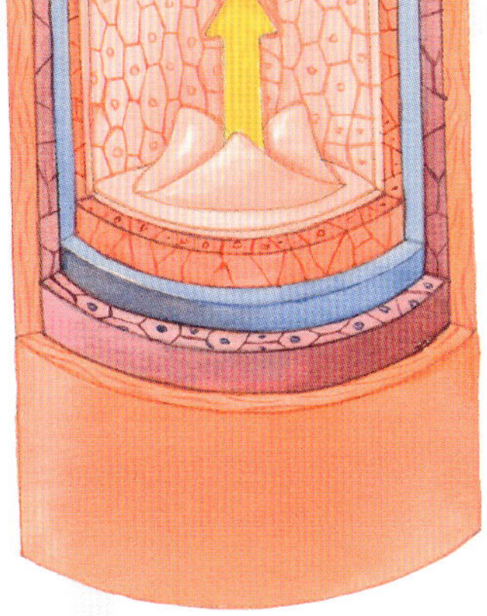
Open valve

Heart valves

Between the atria and the corresponding ventricles are atrio-ventricular valves. The flow of blood going from the ventricles towards the pulmonary arteries and the aorta is controlled by semi lunar valves. Each of these valves regulates its own opening and closing action depending on the differences in pressure on the two sides of the valve. When the pressure is greater on the side where the blood is being propelled, the valve opens. When the pressure returns to zero, it closes and prevents the blood from flowing backwards.

Closed valve
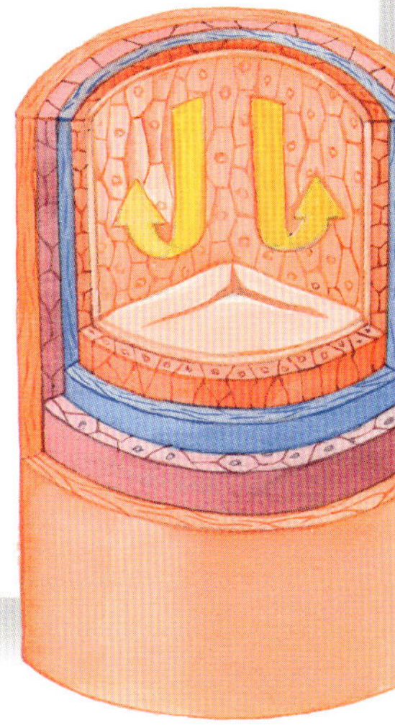

THE CIRCULATION

The heart is divided into two parts by a muscular wall known as the septum. Each part pumps the blood in a distinct circuit, forming the pulmonary circulation and the systemic circulation. These two circuits begin and end in the heart, but always remain separate.

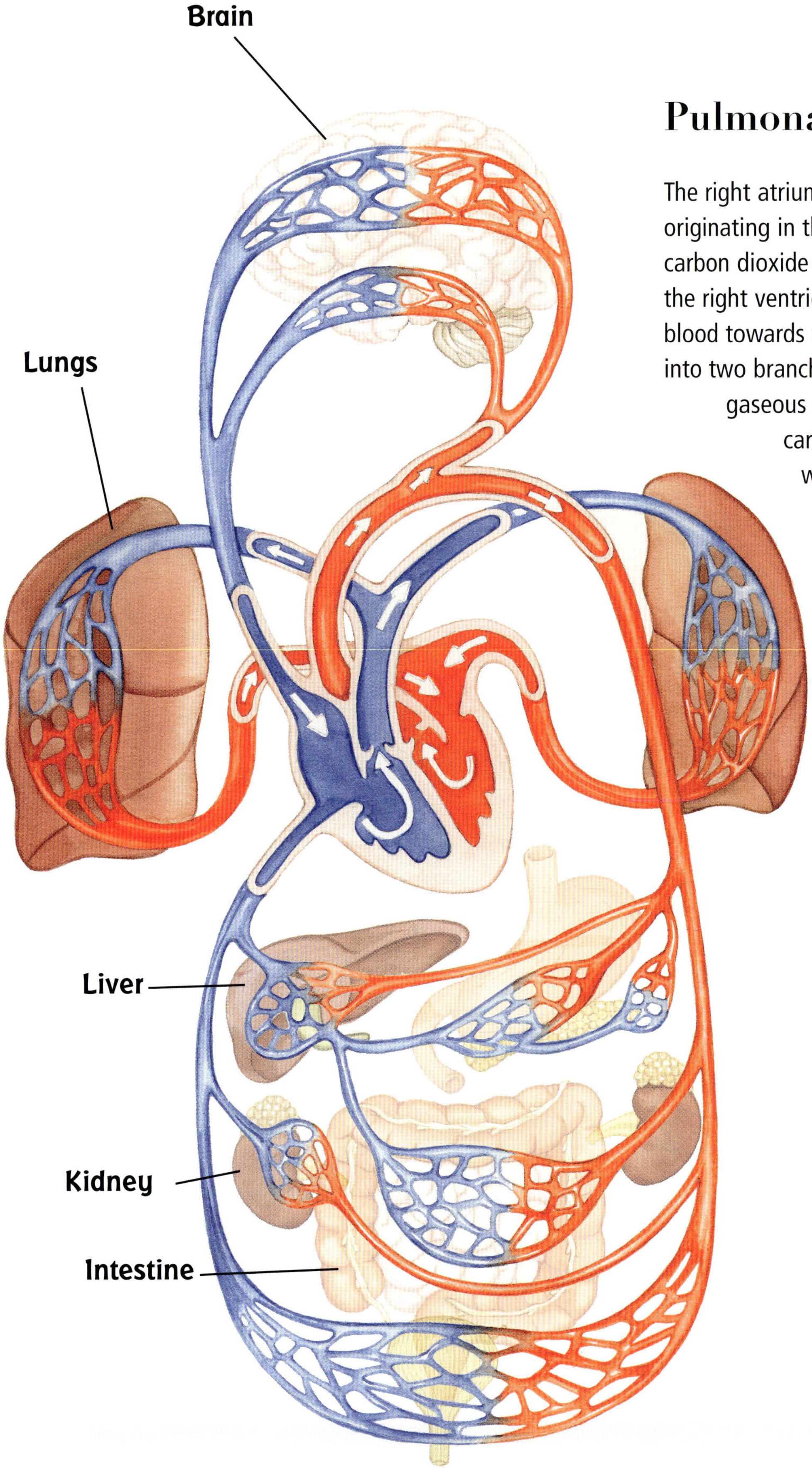

Pulmonary circulation

The right atrium of the heart receives blood from two veins originating in the head and the chest. This blood contains carbon dioxide eliminated by the body's cells. Once it is full, the right ventricle of the heart contracts and pushes the blood towards the pulmonary artery. This large vessel divides into two branches which go to each lung. At this point, gaseous exchange occurs. This consists of extracting carbon dioxide from the blood and replacing it with oxygen before it is pumped back to the left atrium of the heart.

Systemic circulation

The circulation of blood through the body begins on the left side of the heart and ends in the right atrium once it has flowed through all parts of the body. The left ventricle is filled with oxygenated blood coming from the lungs through the atrium located above it. Ventricular contractions create very strong pressure and blood rushes into the aorta, a large collector vessel with smaller arteries going to every part of the body, except the lungs.

Veins

The pressure in the venous system is insufficient to bring the blood back towards the heart. The required pressure is provided by the movement of muscles compressing the veins.

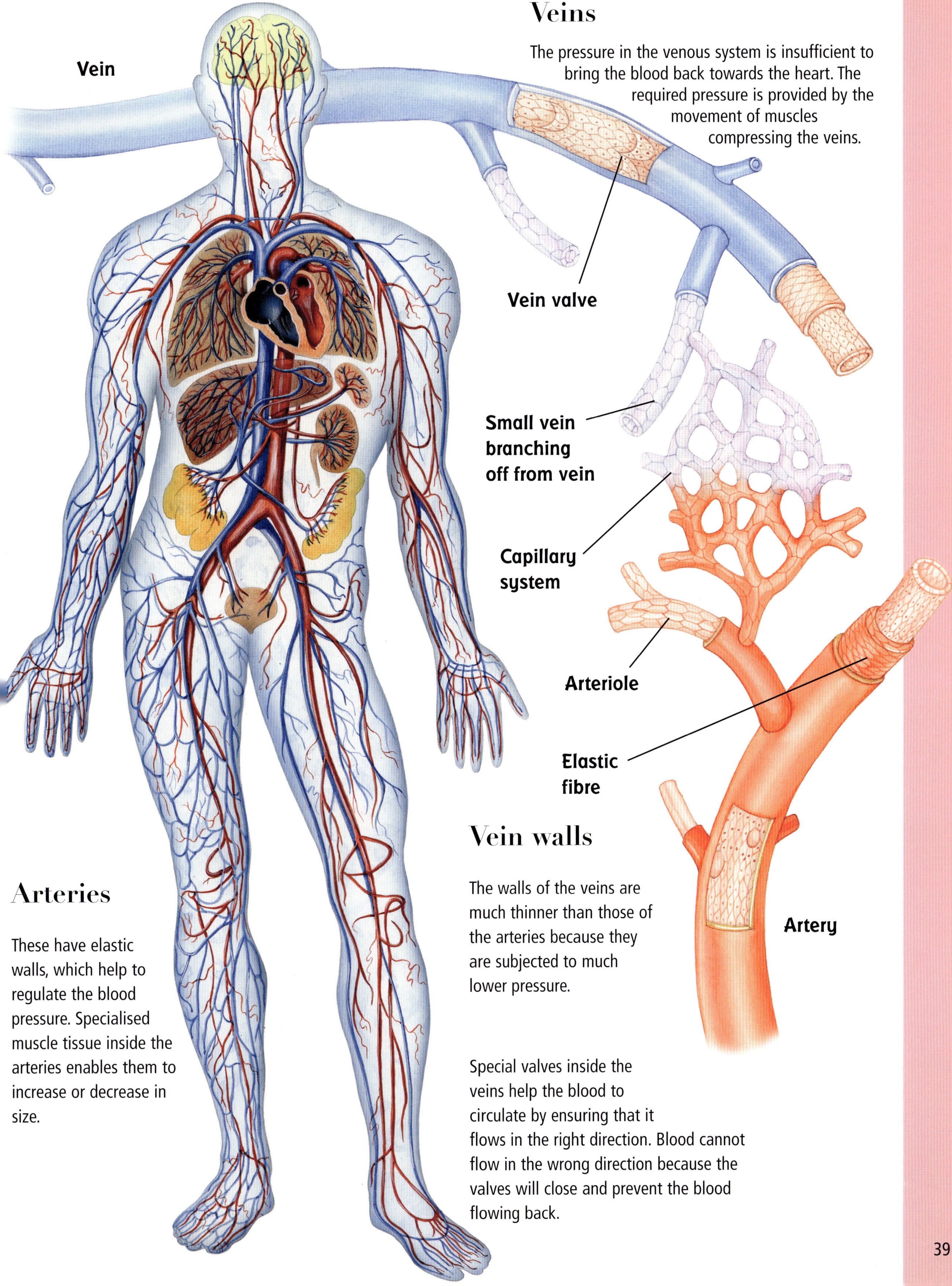

Arteries

These have elastic walls, which help to regulate the blood pressure. Specialised muscle tissue inside the arteries enables them to increase or decrease in size.

Vein walls

The walls of the veins are much thinner than those of the arteries because they are subjected to much lower pressure.

Special valves inside the veins help the blood to circulate by ensuring that it flows in the right direction. Blood cannot flow in the wrong direction because the valves will close and prevent the blood flowing back.

BLOOD

The body of an adult contains about five litres of blood. This fluid transports oxygen and nutrients to the body's cells so that they can carry out their vital functions. Blood has a fluid component called plasma, which contains various types of cells in suspension. Plasma is made up almost solely of water containing dissolved vitamins, proteins, glucose and other substances. The blood cells consist mainly of red blood cells, white blood cells and platelets (involved with blood clotting).

Haemoglobin

Haemoglobin is a special compound of protein and iron. Each red blood cell contains large quantities of these molecules which in turn contain atoms of iron, which are capable of binding to oxygen. When blood passes through the lungs, the haemoglobin captures the oxygen and carries it to the cells, where haemoglobin exchanges oxygen for carbon dioxide.

Haematocrit

The volume of cells in the blood is known as the haematocrit. Under normal conditions, the haematocrit is about 45 per cent of the total blood volume. Red blood cells form the main part of the haematocrit. The white blood cells and platelets represent no more than two per cent of the total cells.

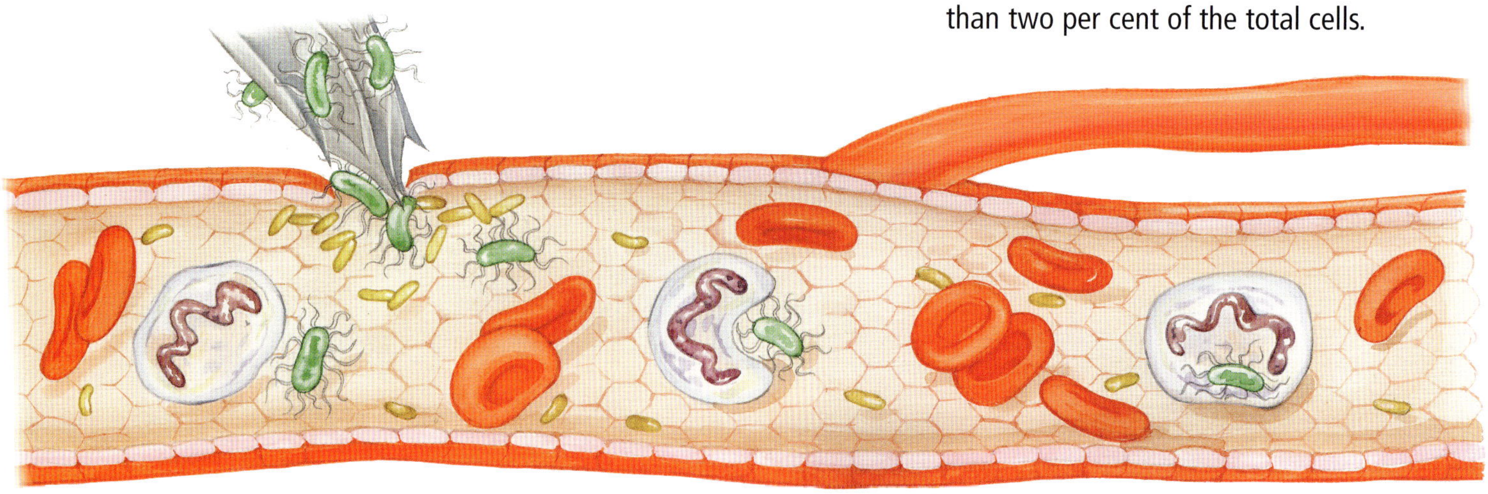

White blood cells

White blood cells guard the body against infection. They are produced by the bone marrow and are larger than the red blood cells. When a foreign body gets into the bloodstream, the white blood cells become active and surround it, and then destroy it. There are various types of white blood cells. Lymphocytes are the only ones that do not surround foreign bodies; they play a special role in the body's immune system.

Platelets

These are produced by the bone marrow and are responsible for stemming bleeding when injury occurs. Whenever a blood vessel is damaged, the platelets begin to aggregate to stop the bleeding, and create threads of fibrin. These filaments control the blood cells by assisting coagulation and closing up the damaged vessel.

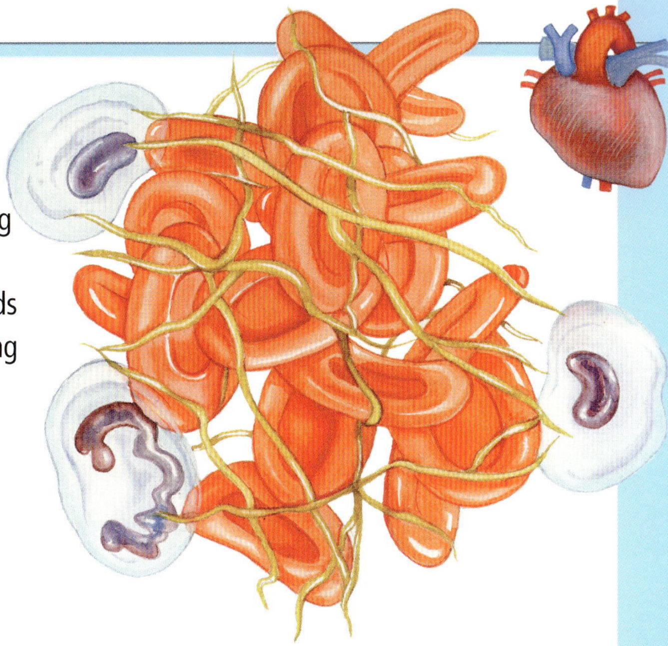

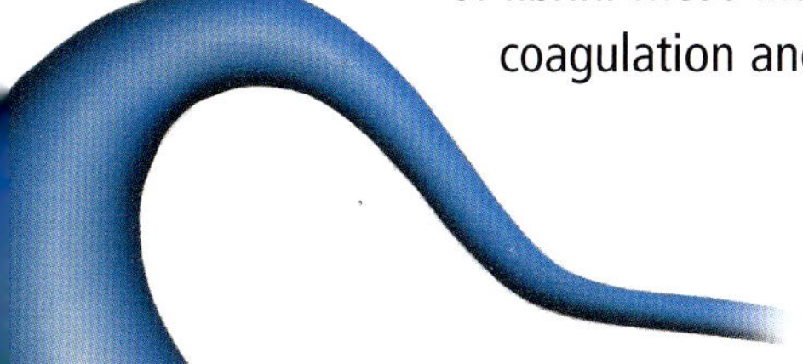

Red blood cells

These special cells have no nucleus. The red blood cells are very small and are able to reach all the body's tissues, transporting haemoglobin containing oxygen. Their life span is rather short (maximum four months). For this reason, the bone marrow is constantly producing new red blood cells to replace the dying ones. If the number of red blood cells is too low, serious health problems such as anaemia may result.

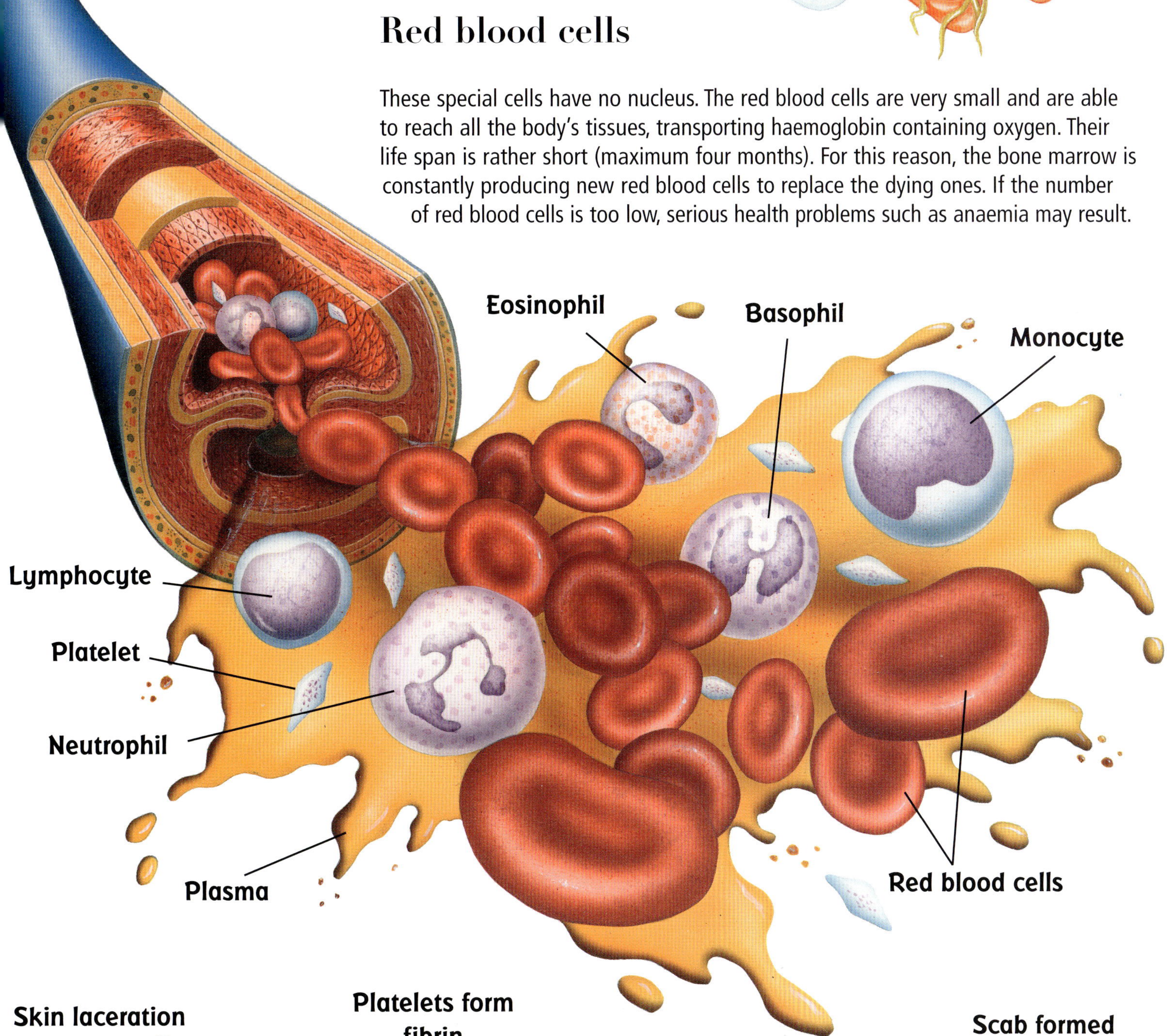

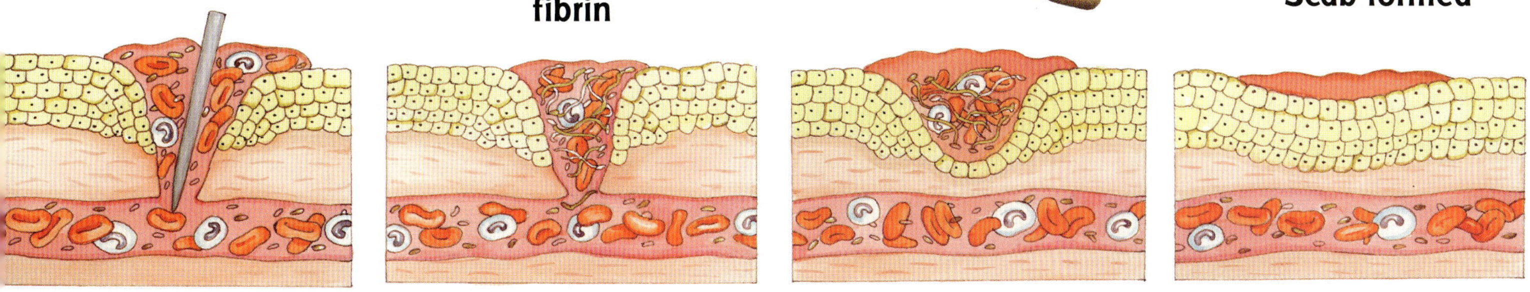

RESPIRATION

Respiration is the exchange of oxygen and carbon dioxide between the atmosphere and all cells of the body, including the lungs. Ventilation is the mechanical process that causes air to enter and exit the lungs. The movement required is produced by the respiratory muscles, which move automatically even while we are asleep. The two stages of breathing are known as inhalation and exhalation.

Vocal cords

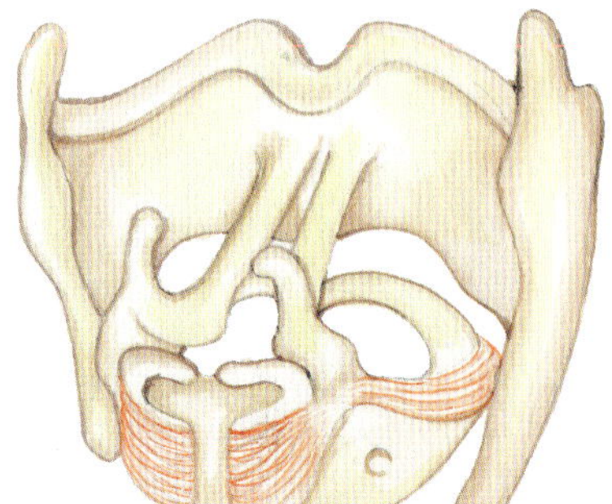

Open

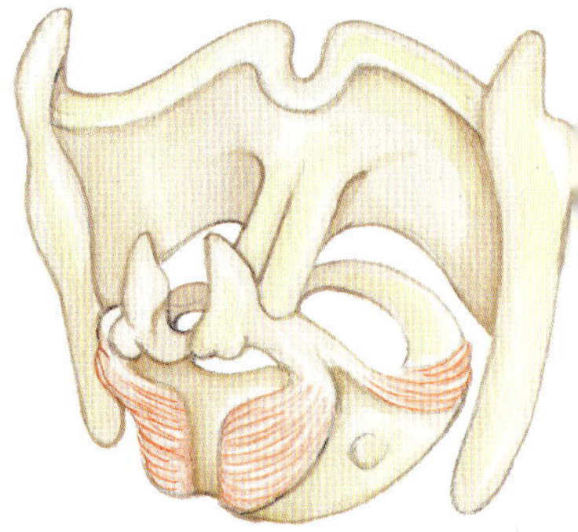

Closed

Voice

Our voice is produced by air passing through the larynx. This organ is located in the throat and contains two folds of cartilage called vocal cords. When we breathe, these cords remain apart, and come together to produce voice sounds. Relaxation or contraction of the muscles that operate these cartilages are controlled by a nerve centre situated in the brain. When the cords come together we emit high-pitched sounds. To produce deeper sounds, the cords must be relaxed. The muscles of the pharynx cause it to function like a sound box in a musical instrument, by creating many different variations.

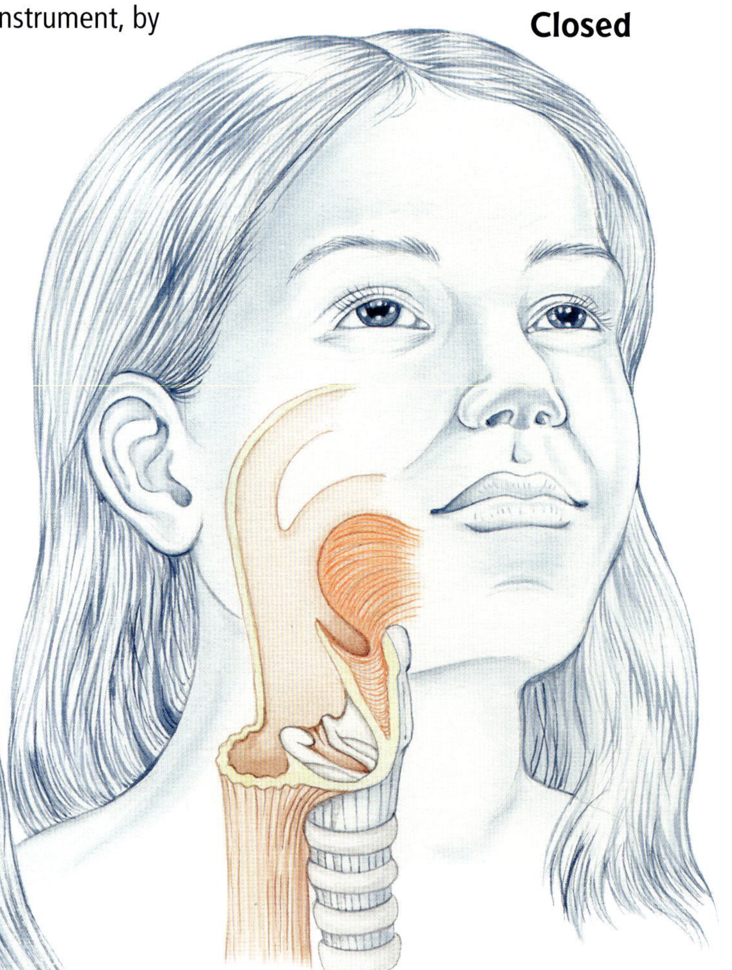

Vocal cords at rest

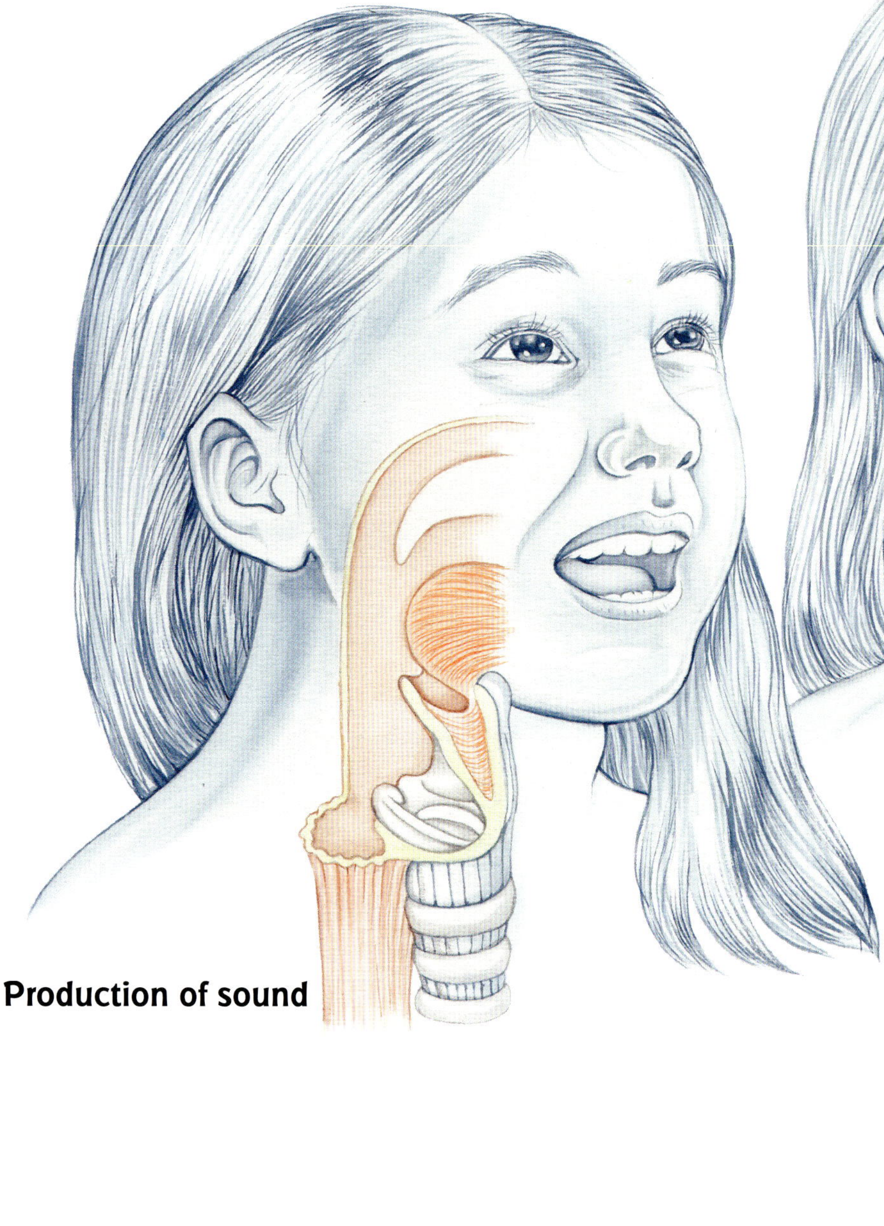

Production of sound

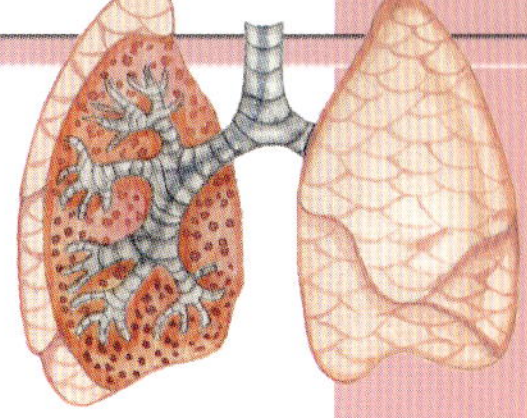

Respiratory system

The main components of the respiratory system are the nose, pharynx, larynx, trachea, bronchi and lungs. Air enters the airways through the nostrils. On entering the nose, it is first filtered by fine hairs which act as a dust filter. Before reaching the delicate pulmonary tissues, the air is once again cleaned and humidified by special cells (the mucosa) in the upper part of the nose. The air then moves down the pharynx and the trachea, and through the bronchi until it reaches the lungs.

Diaphragm

The diaphragm is the principal respiratory muscle. When it contracts and reduces in size, it causes the rib cage to increase in size. When it relaxes, it assumes its normal arched shape and the rib cage contracts.

These two rhythmic movements of the chest are assisted by numerous other muscles situated around the ribs and down the length of the abdomen.

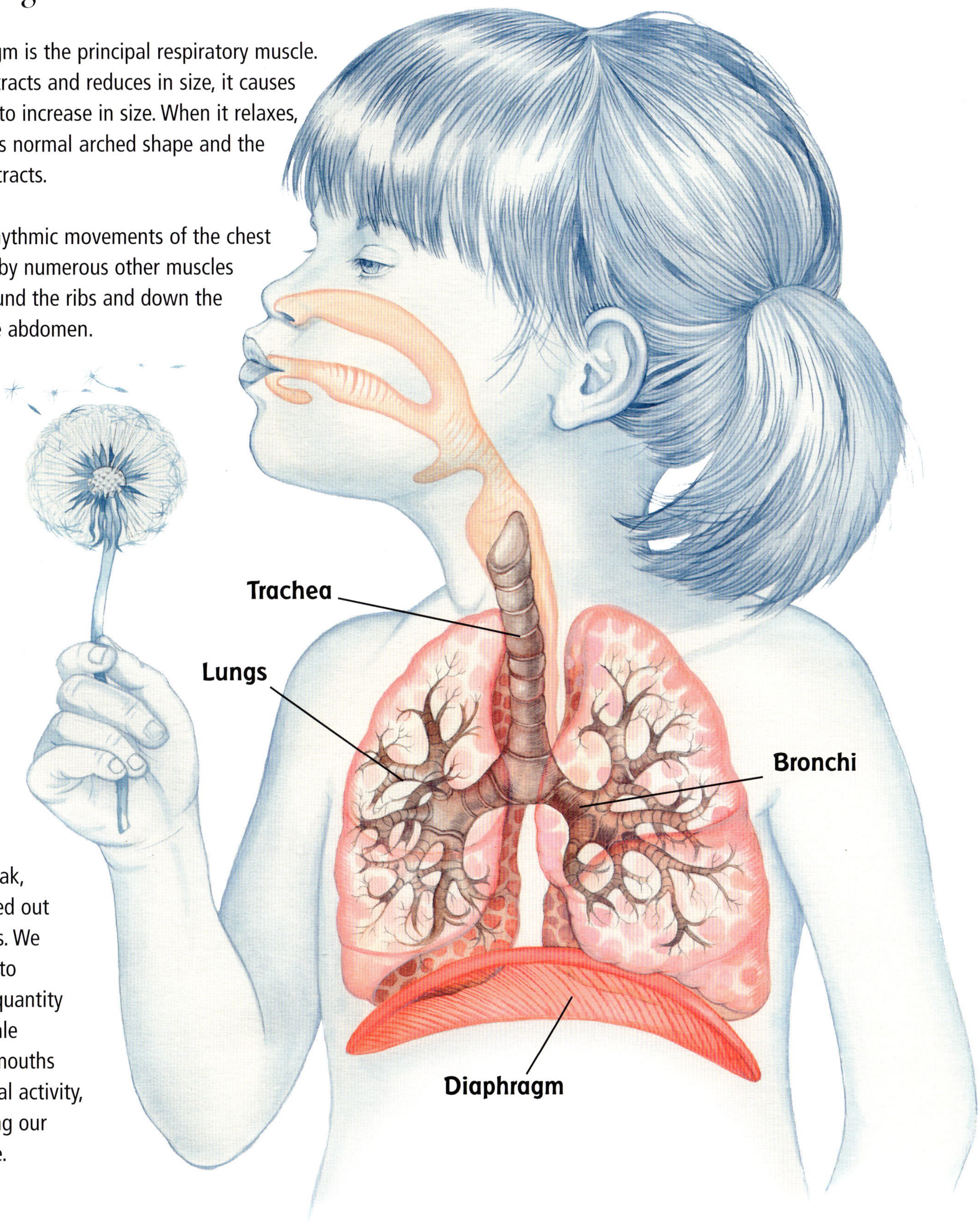

When we speak, air is expressed out of our mouths. We are also able to increase the quantity of air we inhale through our mouths during physical activity, thus increasing our oxygen intake.

THE LUNGS

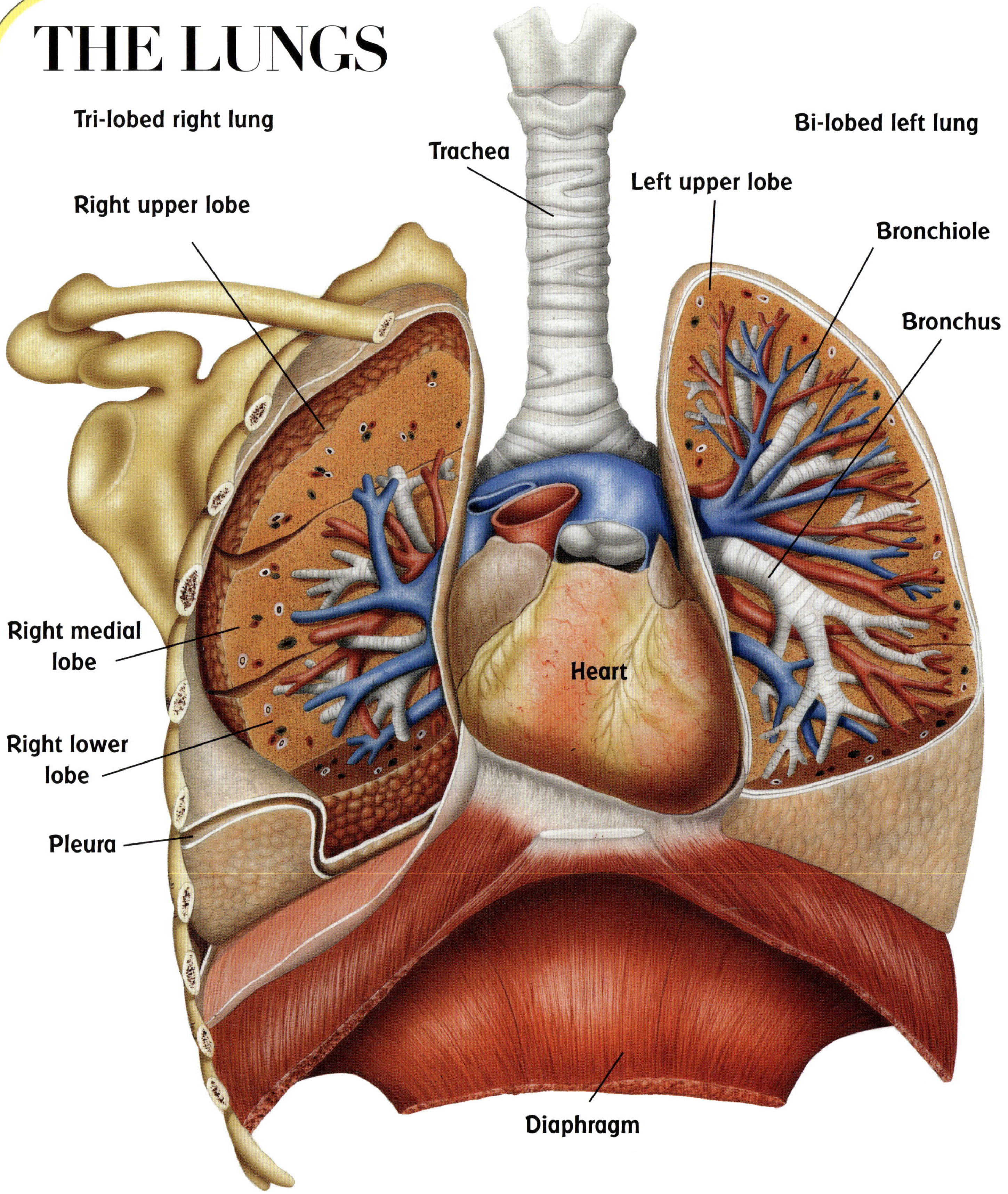

The lungs are a pair of organs found in the upper part of the torso. They share the space inside the thoracic cavity with the heart, and are supported by the respiratory muscle called the diaphragm. They are cone shaped and covered with a fine, strong membrane called the pleura, which protects the delicate spongy internal structure. These two organs are not perfectly symmetrical. The right lung is larger and made up of three lobes. The left lung has only two lobes, leaving more space for the heart. Each lung is connected to one branch of the bronchi, which is in turn divided into thousands of bronchioles ending in alveoli.

OXYGENATION OF THE BLOOD

Alveoli

The lungs contain several hundred million pulmonary alveoli. They are grouped together at the ends of the bronchioles, forming minute bunches surrounded by fine blood vessels. This complex structure produces an increased surface area for gas exchange to occur. Researchers have calculated that the surface area available for oxygenation of the blood is enormous, and is equal to more than 30 times the external surface of the whole body.

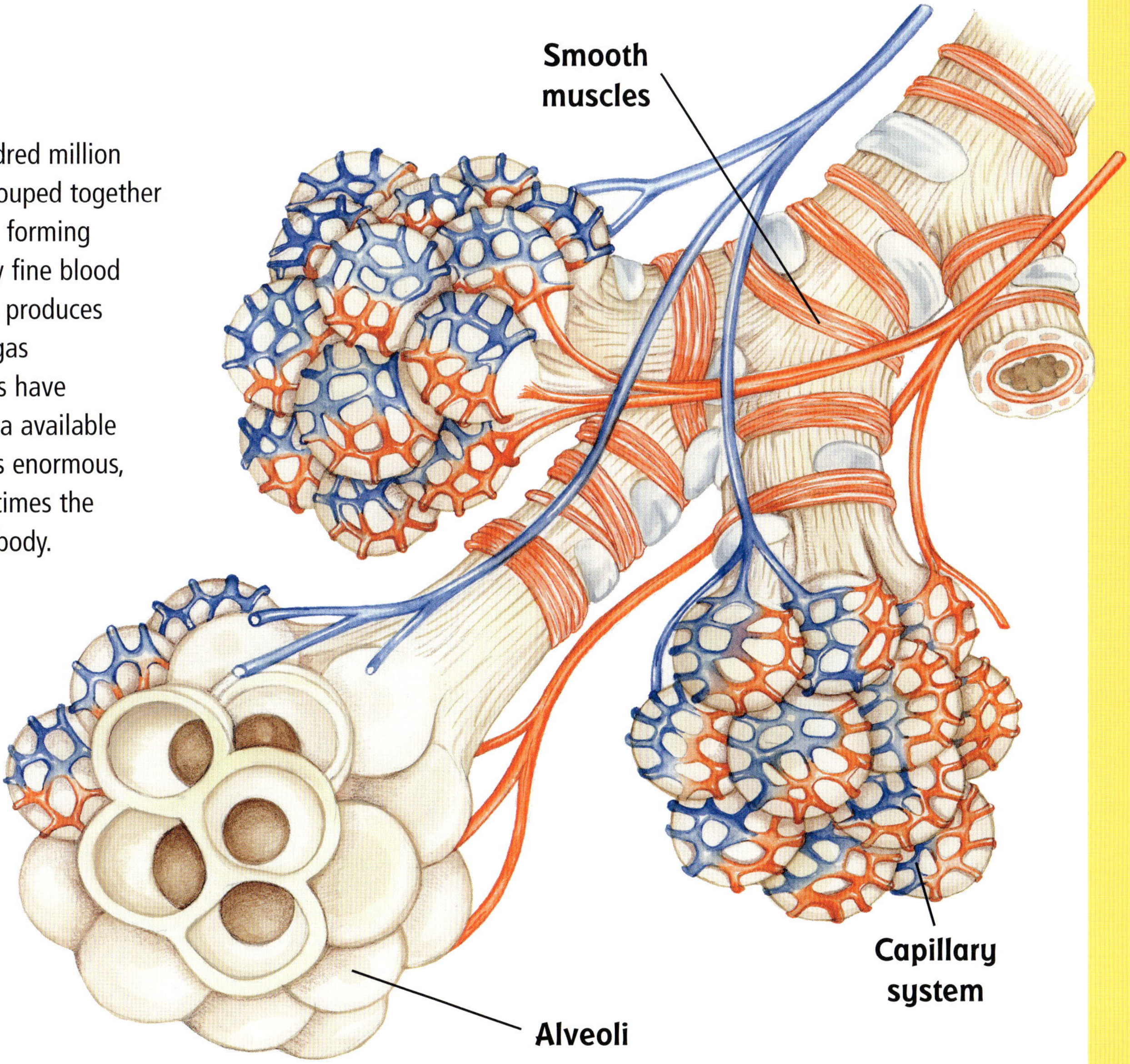

The blood circulating through the capillaries comes into contact with the air contained inside the alveoli. This facilitates contact between the oxygen and the haemoglobin.

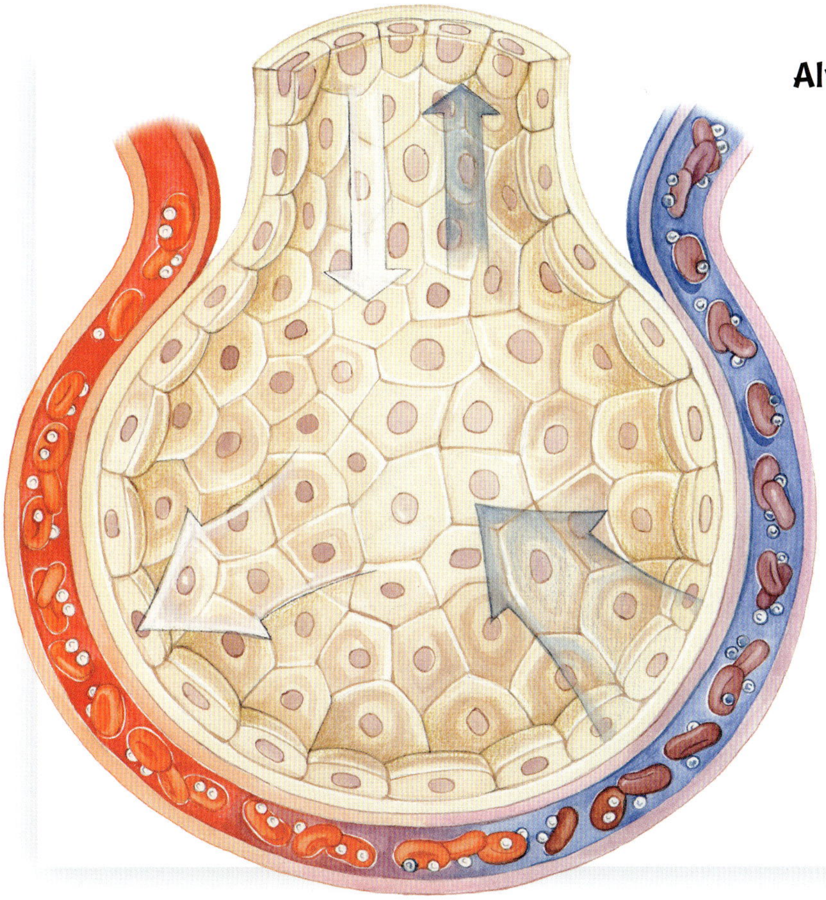

Blood containing carbon dioxide is pumped by the right ventricle of the heart through into the bronchioli. It circulates through the capillaries surrounding the alveoli, leaving behind the carbon dioxide and collecting oxygen from the air inside the lungs. The wall separating the blood from the alveoli is extremely thin and no bigger than the diameter of a cell. The delicate internal tissue of the alveolus is kept moist by a fluid, which protects the walls and prevents them from sticking together.

THE MOUTH AND TEETH

All the cells in our body require constant nutrition. Before nutrients are distributed through the body they undergo a long transformation process in the digestive system. The large molecules contained in our food are broken down into smaller components, which can be used by the body's cells. The first stages of digestion occur in the mouth, where the food is crushed by the teeth and mixed with saliva. Movements of the tongue carry the food between the teeth several times to ensure that each mouthful is properly chewed before it is swallowed.

Teeth

Each tooth is made up of three distinct parts. The crown protrudes out of the gum and is visible inside the mouth. It has a hard enamel coating to protect the dentine and the internal pulp. The neck is the part which is in contact with the gum. The root is the part located deep inside the gum and embedded in the jawbone.

Mastication

There are 32 teeth in an adult mouth divided between the upper and lower jaws. At the back of the mouth are 12 large molar teeth, which are designed to crush food into smaller pieces. In front of them are eight premolars, which are smaller but carry out a very similar task. There are four pointed canine teeth that we use to tear our food. At the front of the mouth are the eight incisors, which we use to cut through food or bite off pieces. These differently shaped teeth are perfectly adapted to the varied food habits of humans.

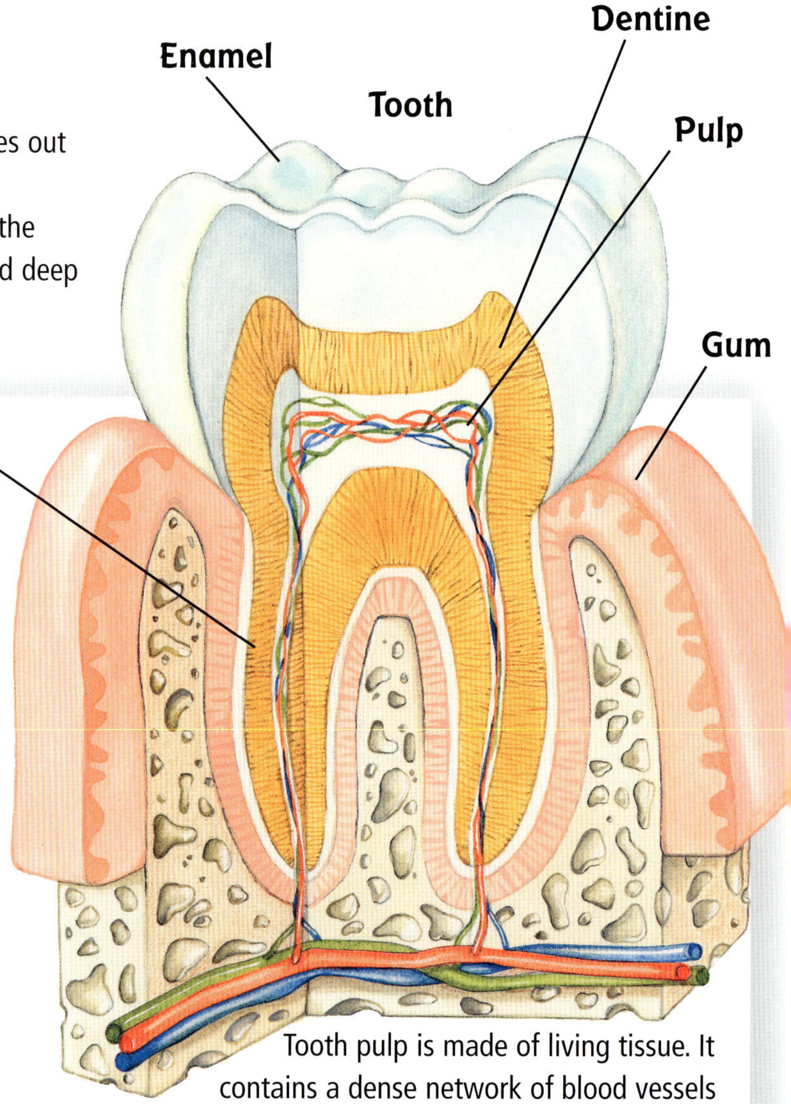

Tooth pulp is made of living tissue. It contains a dense network of blood vessels and tiny nerves, which make our teeth sensitive to pain.

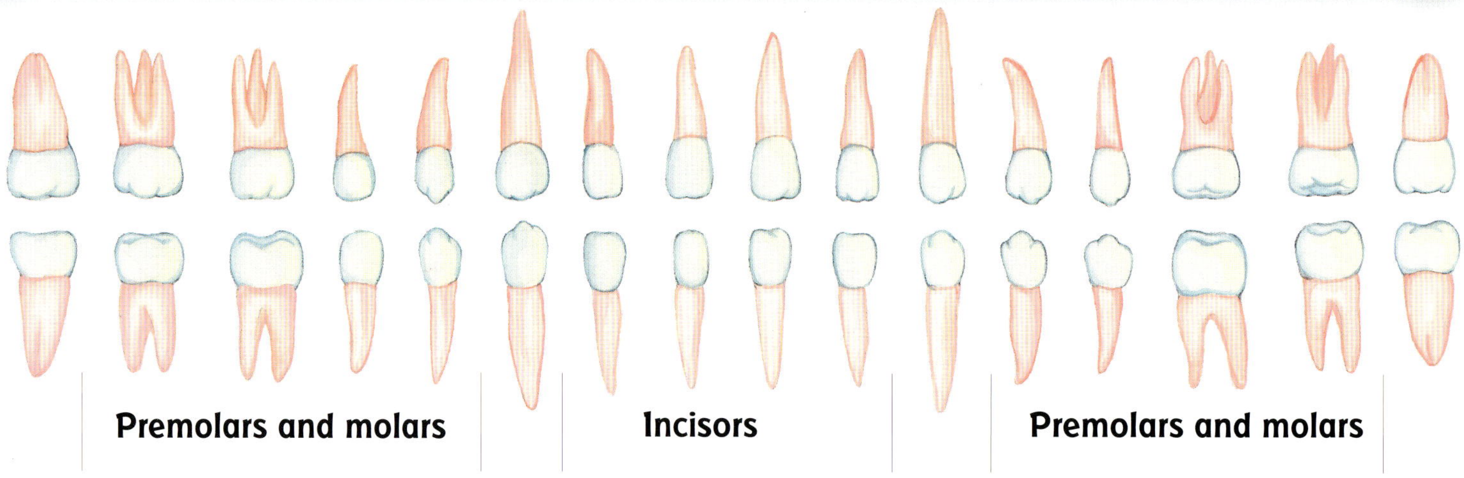

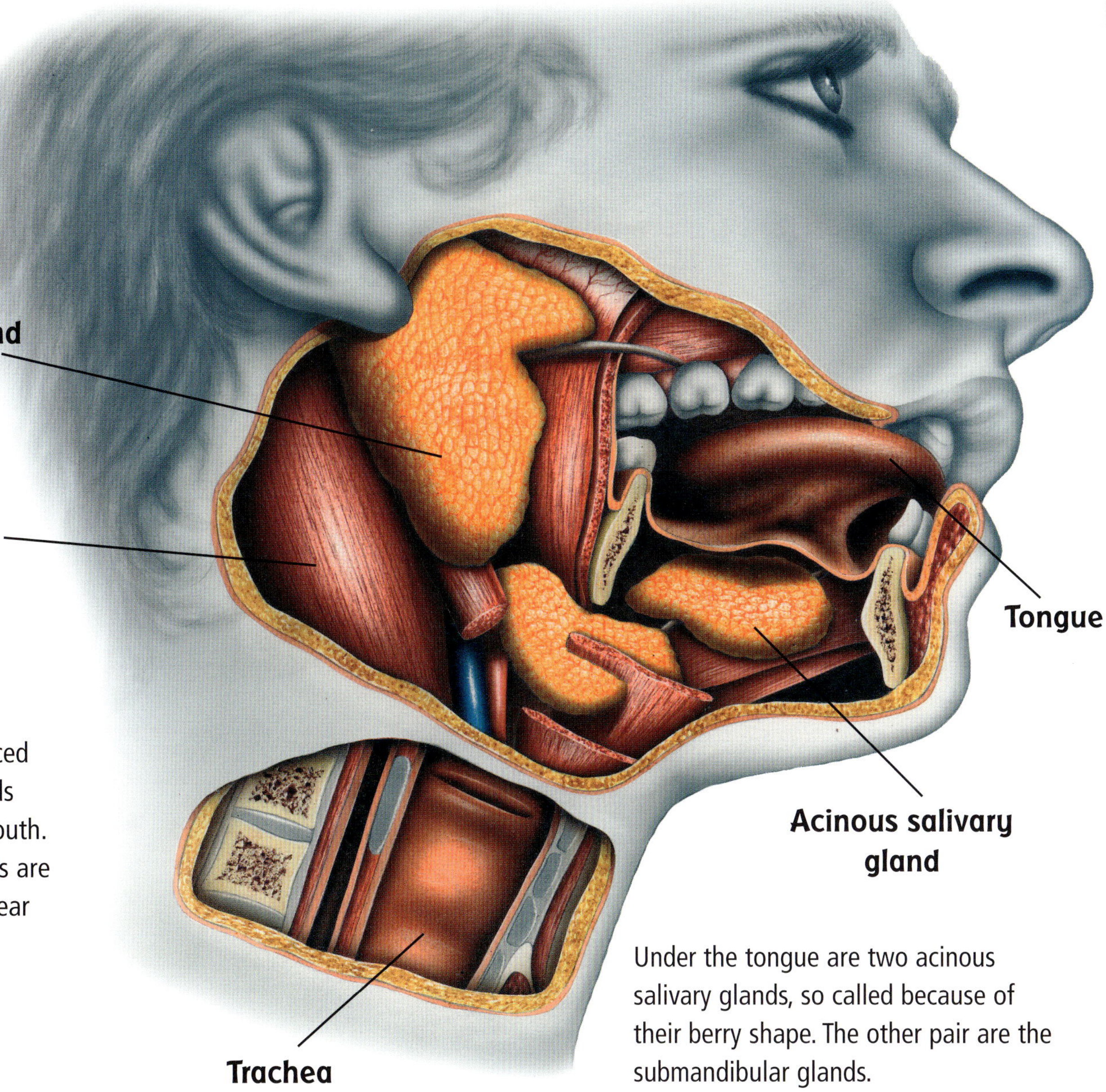

When food is being chewed it mixes with saliva, which is produced by three pairs of glands located around the mouth. The two parotid glands are situated between the ear and the lower jaw (mandible).

Under the tongue are two acinous salivary glands, so called because of their berry shape. The other pair are the submandibular glands.

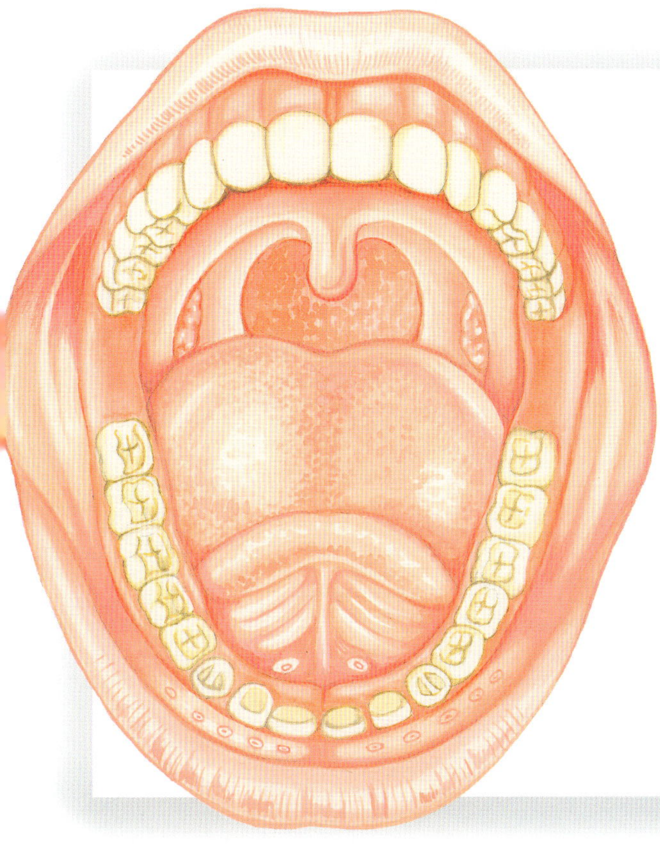

Saliva

The salivary juices consist mainly of water but also contain digestive enzymes. One, called salivary amylase, is capable of beginning to digest starch even while it is still in the mouth. If we chew a piece of bread for a long time we can detect a sweetish taste under the tongue; this comes from the glucose derived from starch. The other salivary fluids serve to soften the chewed food. This mixture resulting from the chewing process is called the food bolus. When swallowed, it moves down through the pharynx and the oesophagus into the stomach.

DIGESTION

The stomach is a part of the digestive tract located in the abdomen and linked to the mouth by the oesophagus, also known as the gullet. When the stomach is empty and at rest, the lining contains tiny folds. During digestion, these dilate to form a pouch able to hold more than three litres of food bolus. The process of digestion lasts for several hours. During this time, the bolus is mixed with the gastric juices produced by glands located in the stomach lining. The gastric juices contain hormones and enzymes which assist the digestive process. They also contain hydrochloric acid, which helps digestion by activating the enzyme pepsin.

LOS and pylorus

Movement of the food bolus inside the stomach is controlled by two muscles called the lower oesophageal sphincter (LOS) and the pylorus. The LOS is located at the entrance, like a gatekeeper, and prevents the reflux of food back up the oesophagus. The pylorus controls movement of the bolus towards the small intestine and prevents it arriving there before it is properly digested.

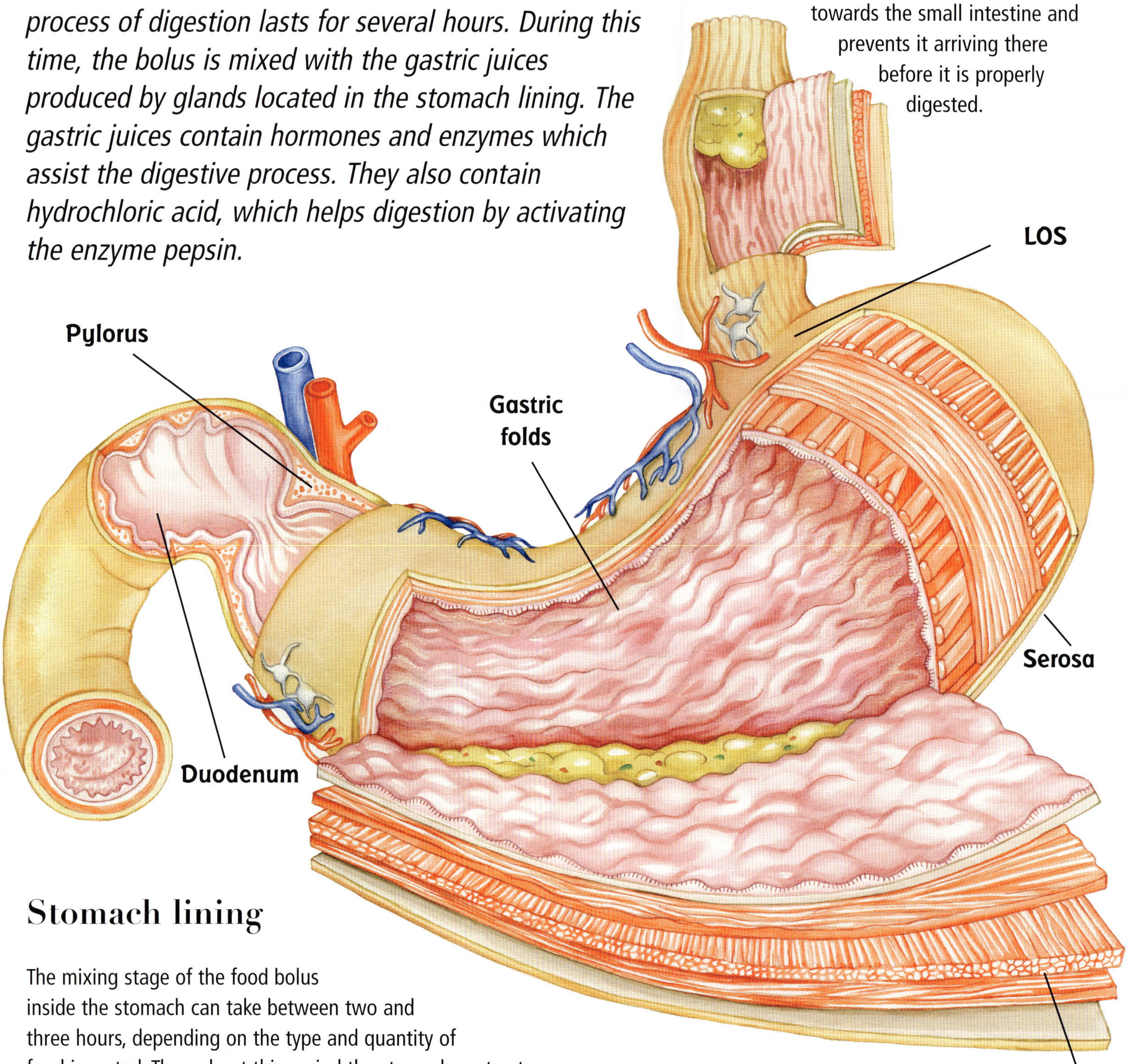

Stomach lining

The mixing stage of the food bolus inside the stomach can take between two and three hours, depending on the type and quantity of food ingested. Throughout this period the stomach contracts rhythmically via three distinct layers of muscle in the wall, which are arranged in circular lengthwise and crosswise fashion. This mechanical movement of the stomach allows the bolus to be processed. Once partly digested by the gastric juices, the bolus becomes chyme and is ready to enter the intestine.

Digestive tract

Each of the different stages of the digestive tract plays an important role in the transformation of foodstuffs.

Mouth: chewing, or mastication, is the process of breaking up food and mixing it with saliva.

Salivary glands: produce saliva containing digestive enzymes.

Stomach: mixing of the food bolus, partial digestion and elimination of many micro-organisms which may present a danger to health.

Small intestine: digestion of food and absorption of vitamins and minerals.

Large intestine: absorption of the final remaining nutrients, water and ions before elimination of waste from the body.

Liver: production of bile and other enzymes necessary for digestion.

Gall bladder: storage of bile waiting to be used.

Pancreas: production of digestive enzymes.

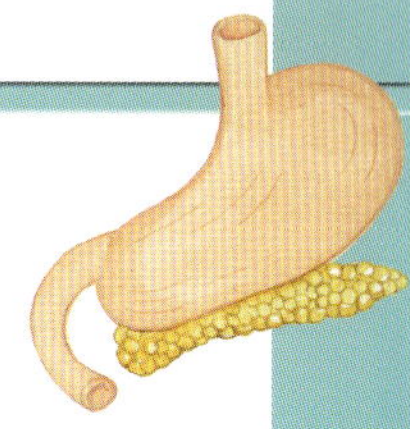

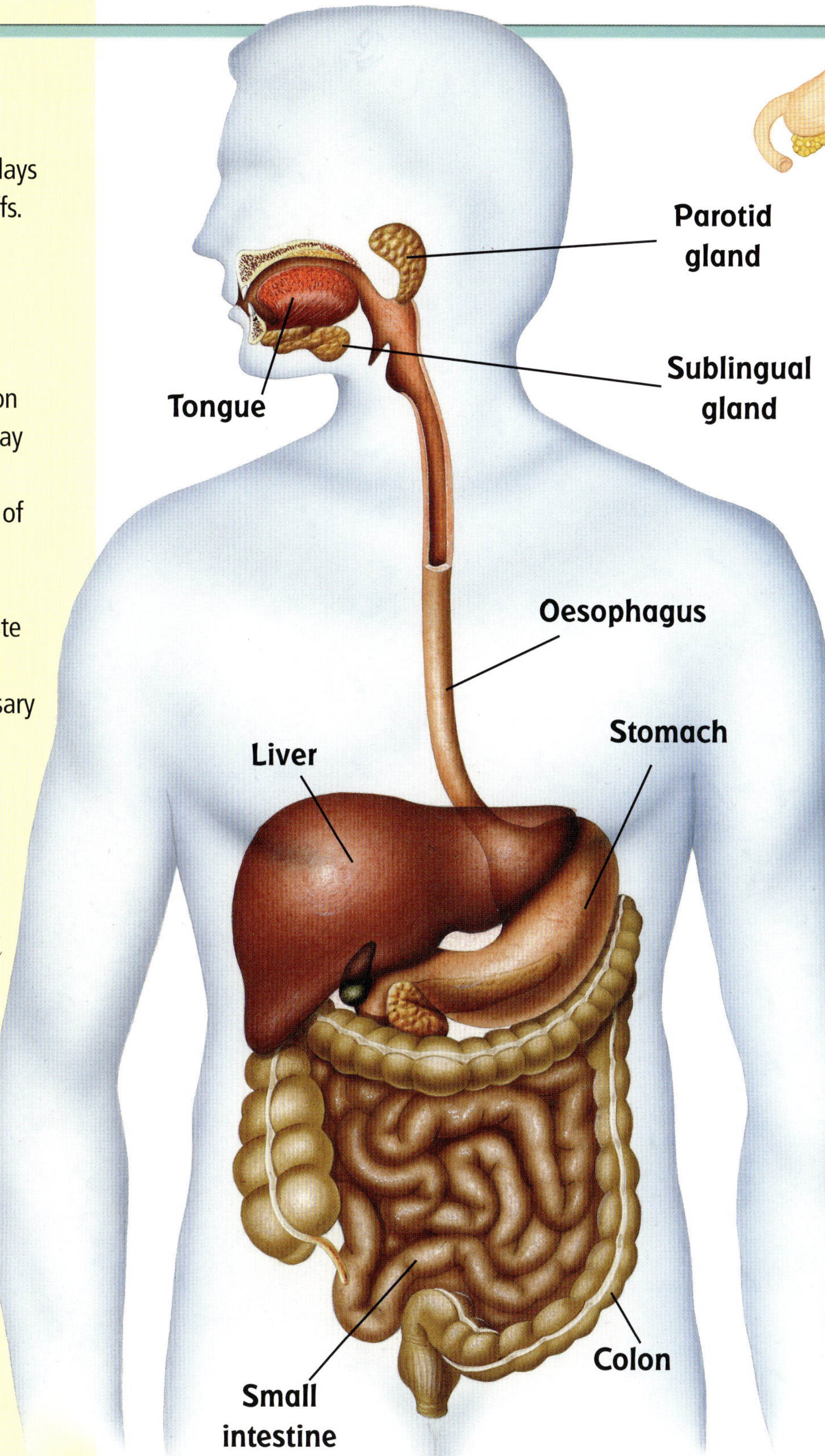

Lining of the digestive tract

The lining of the digestive tract consists of successive layers of tissue known as tunica. The different sections of the digestive tract have various shapes depending on their functions. On the outside is a layer of smooth muscle which covers the tissue forming the sub-mucosa. The internal layer is formed from epithelial tissue, which also differs greatly from one segment of the digestive tract to another. Both the stomach and the intestine are coated with an additional external serosa which facilitates their movements.

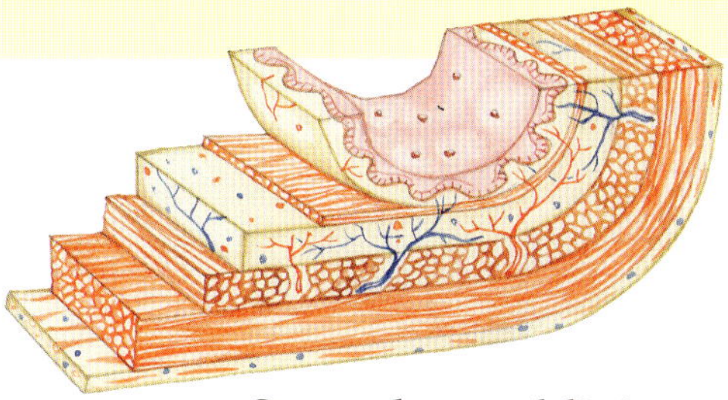

Oesophageal lining

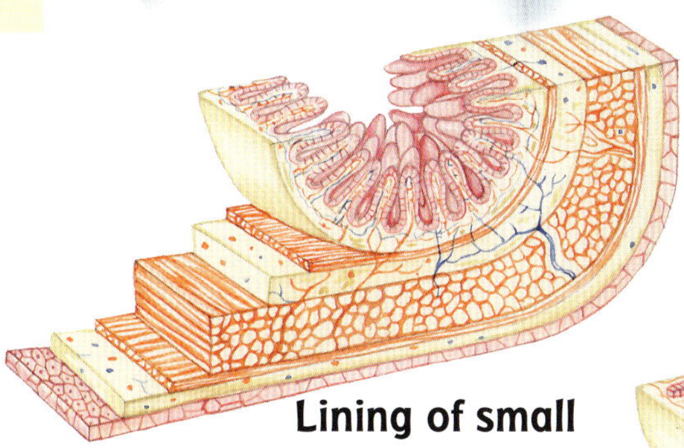

Lining of small intestine

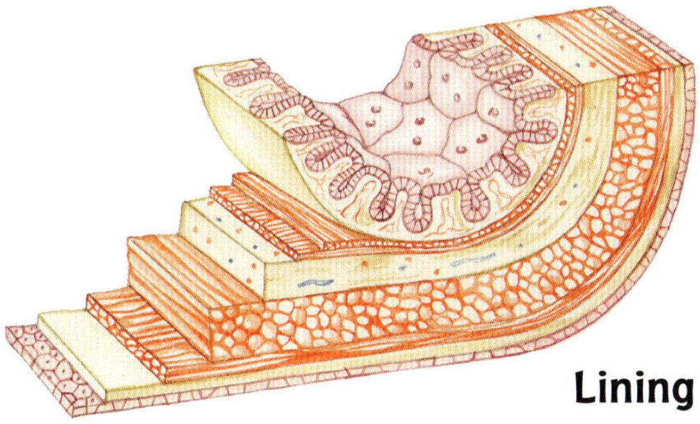

Lining of stomach

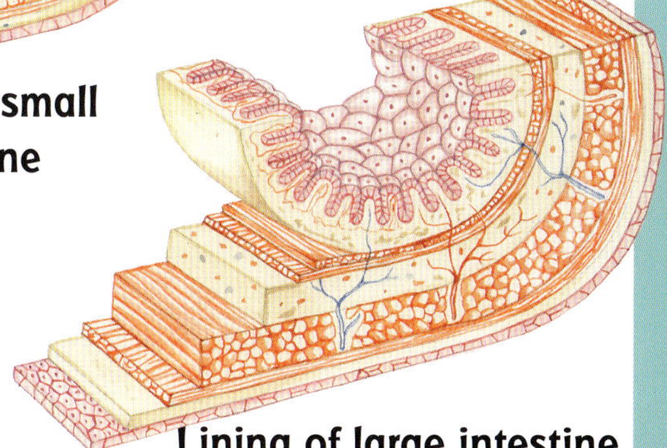

Lining of large intestine

THE INTESTINE, LIVER AND PANCREAS

The first part of the intestine is the small intestine. It may measure up to seven metres and its diameter varies from three to five centimetres. It consists of three sections: the duodenum, jejunum and ileum. Bile and other enzymes secreted by the pancreas flow into the duodenum, the segment closest to the stomach. These combine with the enteric juices produced by the intestinal mucosa. They facilitate the final preparation of chyle (chyme mixed with water), which is then ready to be absorbed in the small intestine.

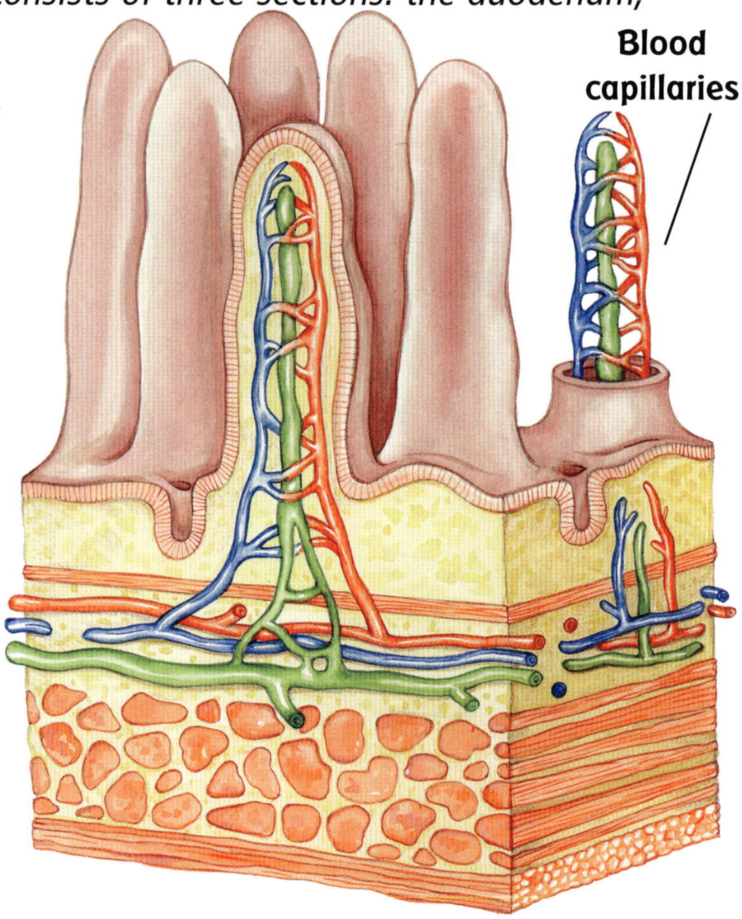

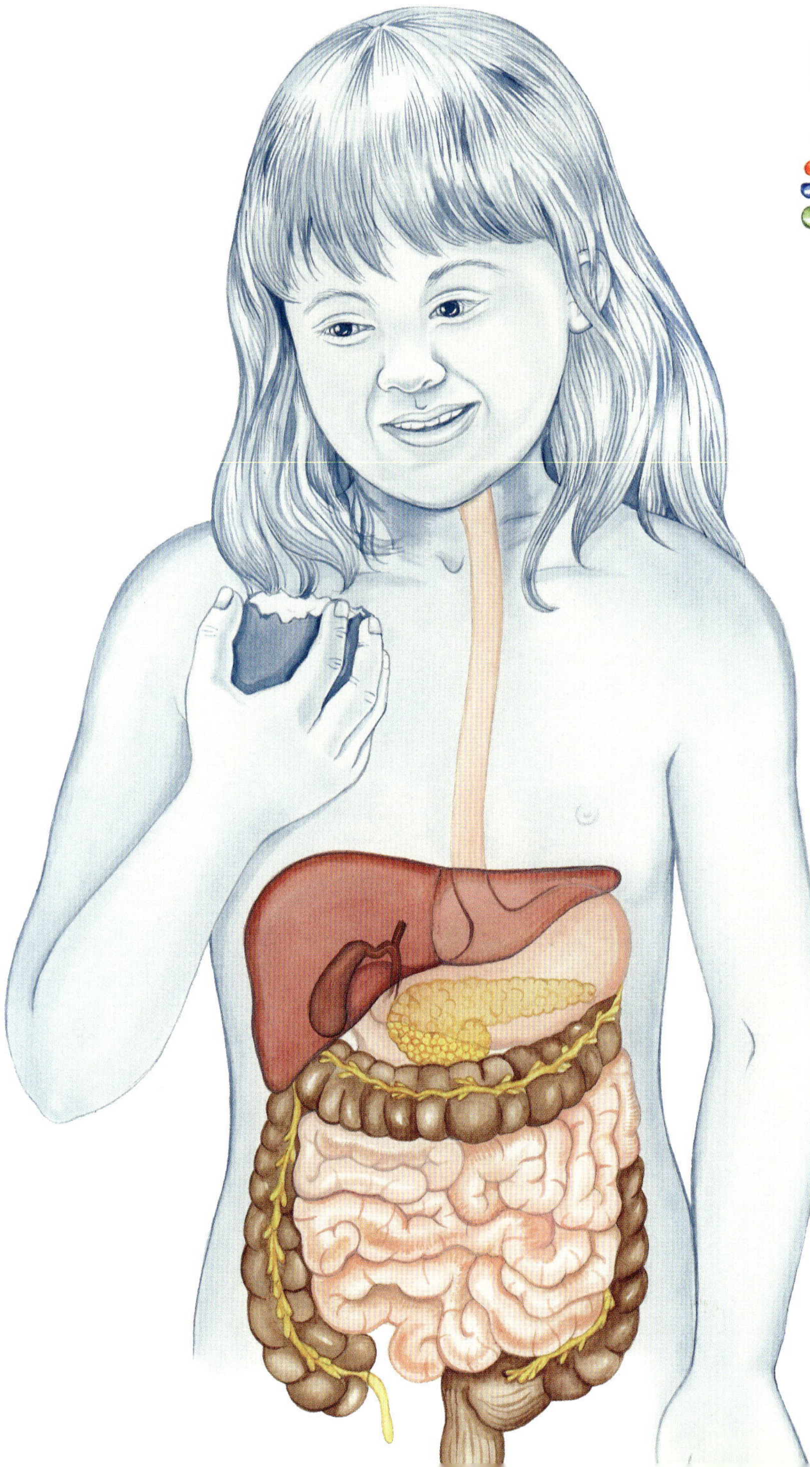

The large intestine is subdivided into three sections: the cæcum, colon and rectum. Its total length is one and a half metres and its diameter may measure up to eight or nine centimetres. It completes the process of absorbing water and mineral salts before sending any undigested substances to be eliminated from the body.

Intestinal villi

Inside the small intestine are small finger-shaped projections known as intestinal villi. Their presence increases the surface area able to absorb the nutrients contained in the chyme. Special cells on the outside of the villi facilitate exchange between the blood and the lymph flowing through the dense network of blood vessels.

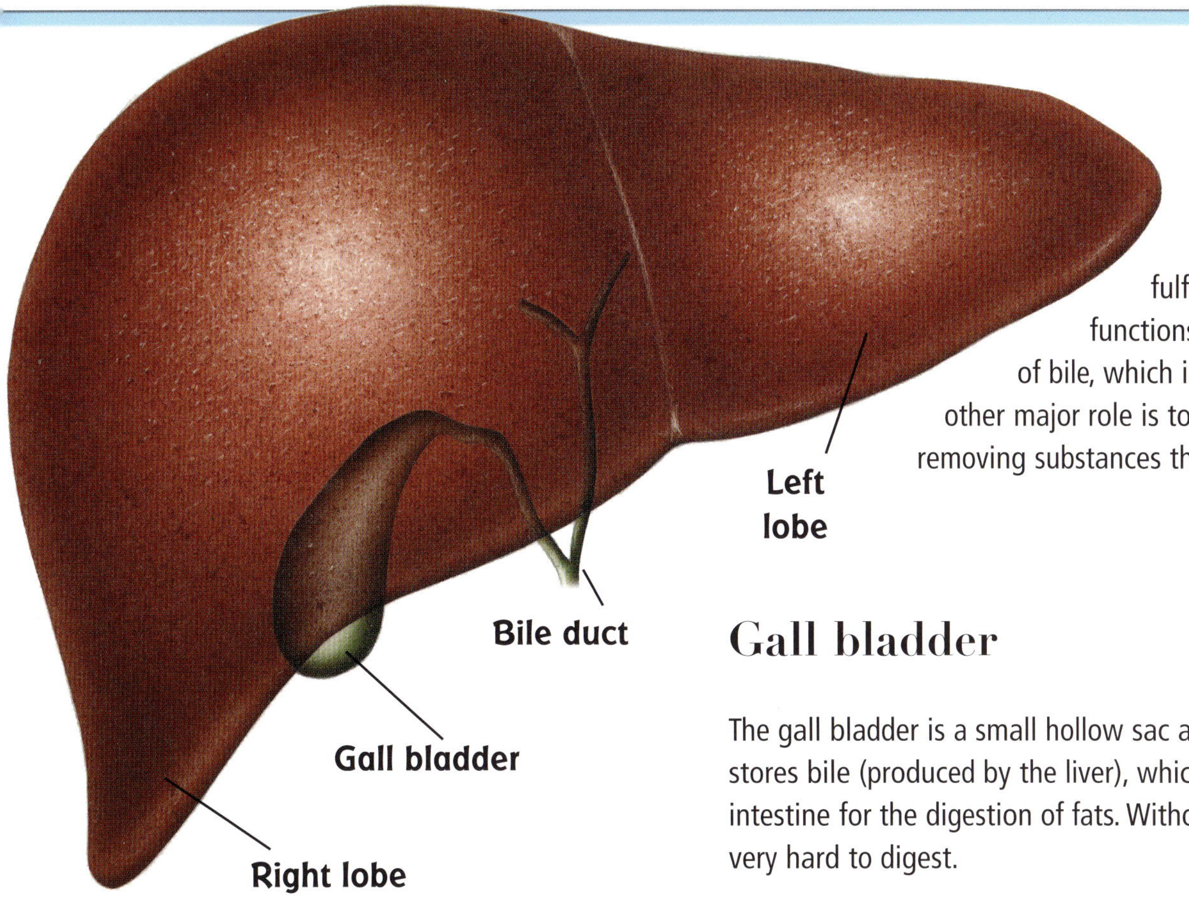

Liver

The liver is the largest gland in the human body. It fulfils a number of important functions, including the production of bile, which is essential for digestion. Its other major role is to purify the blood by removing substances that are toxic to the body.

Gall bladder

The gall bladder is a small hollow sac attached to the bile duct. It stores bile (produced by the liver), which is ready to join the small intestine for the digestion of fats. Without bile, fatty foods would be very hard to digest.

Pancreas

The pancreas is a gland with two functions. It produces pancreatic juices rich in ions and enzymes, which are able to digest proteins, carbohydrates and triglycerides. It also produces the hormone insulin, which controls the quantity of glucose in our blood.

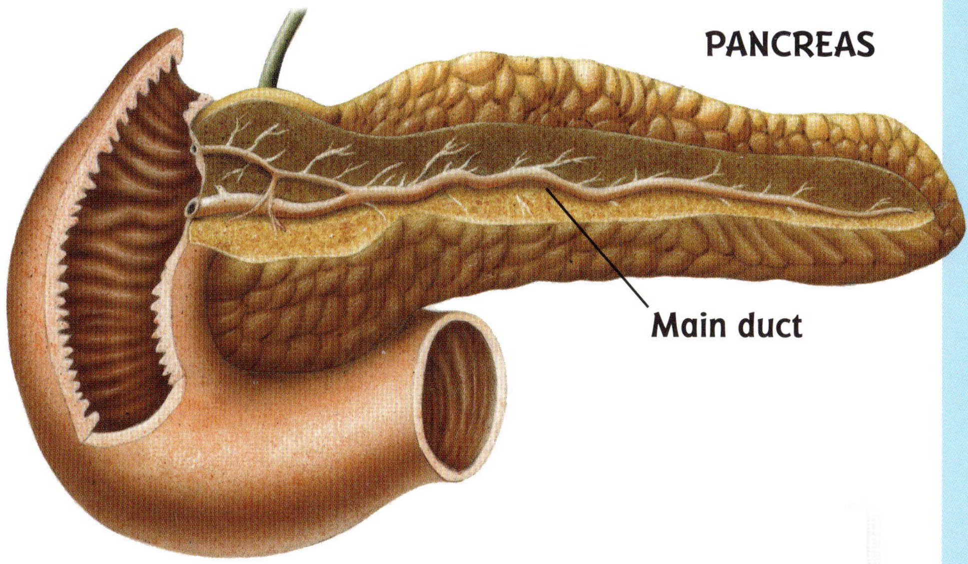

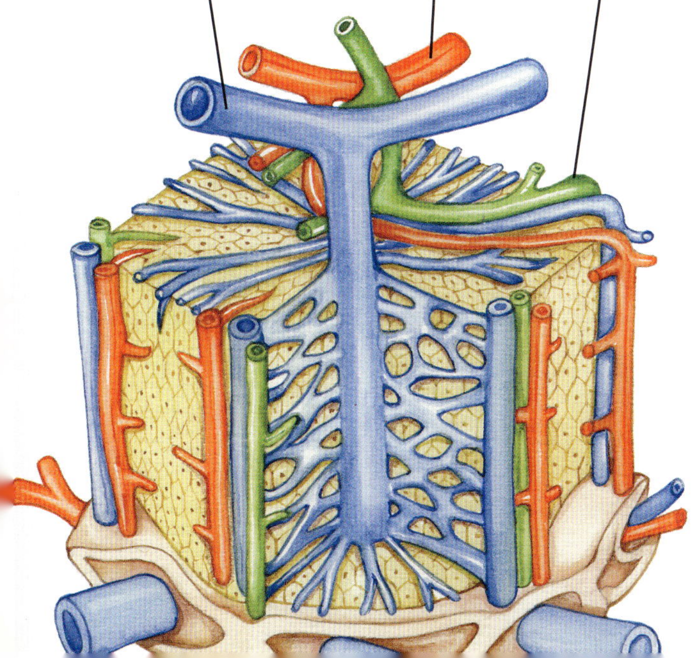

Hepatic lobule

The liver comprises thousands of tiny lobules. Despite their small size, each one has its own highly complex circulatory system. They receive blood directly from the intestine via the portal vein. Inside the lobules, substances absorbed during digestion are transformed. A portion of the fats and amino acids is stored in the liver as energy reserves, while other substances are returned to the bloodstream.

NUTRITION

Nutrition is essential for the human body to function. The basic materials required to build new tissue and supply the energy vital for our daily activities are manufactured from carbohydrates, fats and protein. In addition to food, our bodies need minerals, water and vitamins.

Vitamins

Our body needs vitamins if we are to grow and stay healthy. Vitamin D is the only vitamin that can be produced by the body, whereas all the others are extracted from food. They can be absorbed in water (vitamin C and the B group vitamins) or in fats (vitamins A, D, E and K).

Vitamin A

This assists with cell growth, protects us from infection and plays an important role in eyesight. It is found in carrots, spinach, animal liver and eggs.

Vitamin B

There are more than 15 types of vitamins in the B group, and these are indispensable for the production of red blood cells. They are found in cereals, liver, green vegetables and eggs.

Vitamin C

This serves to manufacture connective tissue and helps to heal wounds. We find it in citrus fruits and green vegetables.

Vitamin D

This regulates the absorption of calcium by the bones and is most important for growth. The main supply is found in fish, egg yolks and liver.

Vitamin E

This protects the cell membranes and contributes to the production of haemoglobin. Vegetable oils contain large quantities of this vitamin.

Vitamin K

This is required to produce a substance called prothrombin, which is essential for blood coagulation. We find it in certain green vegetables, but mostly it is produced by intestinal bacteria.

Carbohydrates

Carbohydrates form the main part of our diet. They are found in the starches and sugars contained in bread, cereals, potatoes and milk and are our main source of energy.

The food pyramid

The food pyramid represents the various foodstuffs that should form the basis of our daily nutrition. A healthy diet should be varied. It should also strike a good balance in terms of quantities of the different food types. At the base of the pyramid are the foods that provide carbohydrates for energy. Leafy green vegetables and fruits are a good source of vitamins, while meats, pulses, such as peas, beans or lentils, and cheese contribute protein and vitamins from the B group. At the tip of the pyramid we find the foods containing the most fats. They are also necessary in our diet, but we must be careful to eat only small quantities of these.

Proteins

Proteins supply the raw materials needed to manufacture body tissue. Proteins are large molecules that are broken down into amino acids by our metabolism. The liver then completes the task by converting them into specialised proteins, which can also become a source of energy when our bodies are deprived of carbohydrates.

Fats

Lipids, also known as fats, are reserves of energy which accumulate to form adipose tissue. Rich sources of fats are dairy products, oils and meats.

THE LYMPHATIC SYSTEM

The lymphatic system is a complex network of vessels that collect and carry fluid from the tissues to the circulation, helping to maintain the body's fluid balance. Lymph is made when plasma, the liquid component of blood, leaks from the capillaries (very small blood vessels) into the surrounding tissue spaces where it mixes with the fluid that is present there. Most of this watery fluid returns to the capillaries but the excess (about one to two litres each day) is collected by the lymphatic vessels, filtered by the lymph nodes to remove bacteria and other unwanted material, and then emptied via lymphatic ducts into the bloodstream through large veins near the sides of the neck.

Another important role of the lymphatic system is to maintain the body's immune defences. The lymph nodes, spleen, thymus, bone marrow and tonsils are called lymphoid or lymphatic tissues. They are rich in lymphocytes, the white blood cells that fight invasion by bacteria, viruses and other organisms that can invade the body.

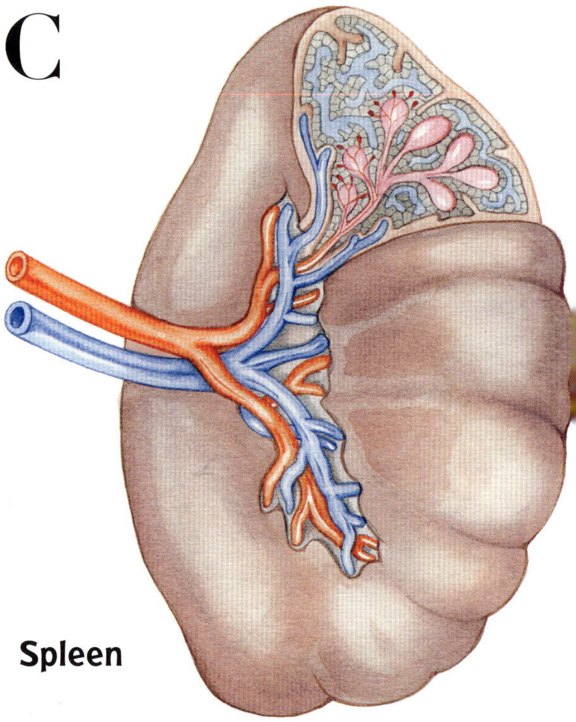

Spleen

The spleen is a small organ that performs two very important functions. It helps to regulate the quantity of blood circulating in the system. It also prepares type B lymphocytes for their defensive role.

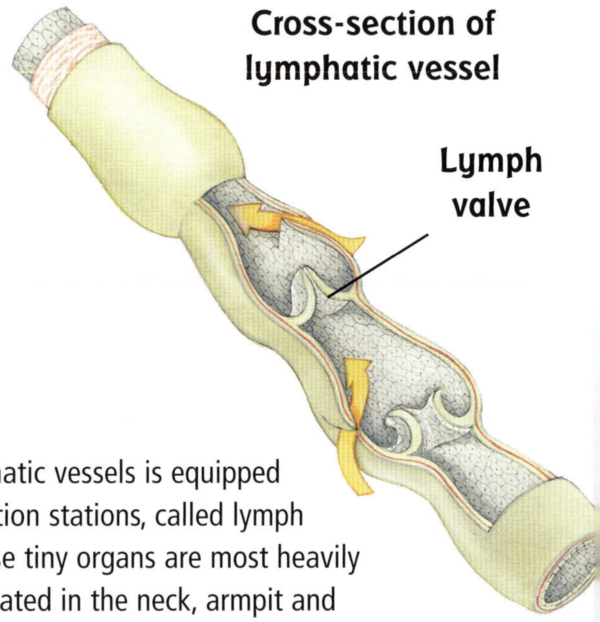

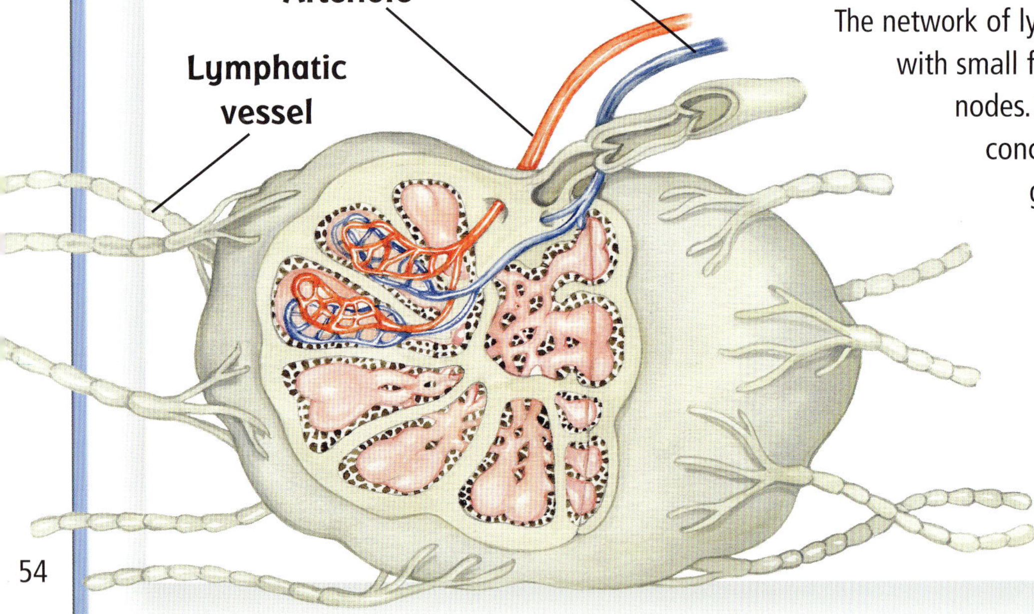

The network of lymphatic vessels is equipped with small filtration stations, called lymph nodes. These tiny organs are most heavily concentrated in the neck, armpit and groin. They are especially designed to store lymphocytes, or white blood cells, which combat any micro-organisms which may get into our tissues. If infection occurs, the lymphatic tissues become inflamed and swollen.

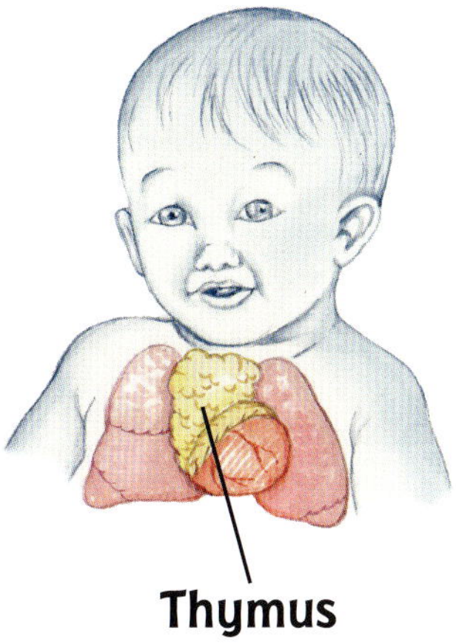

Thymus

Type T killer and T helper lymphocytes mature in the thymus. This organ functions very well during pregnancy and infancy, by protecting us from disease. As the years pass, it tends to shrink and become less active, thus making us more susceptible to infection.

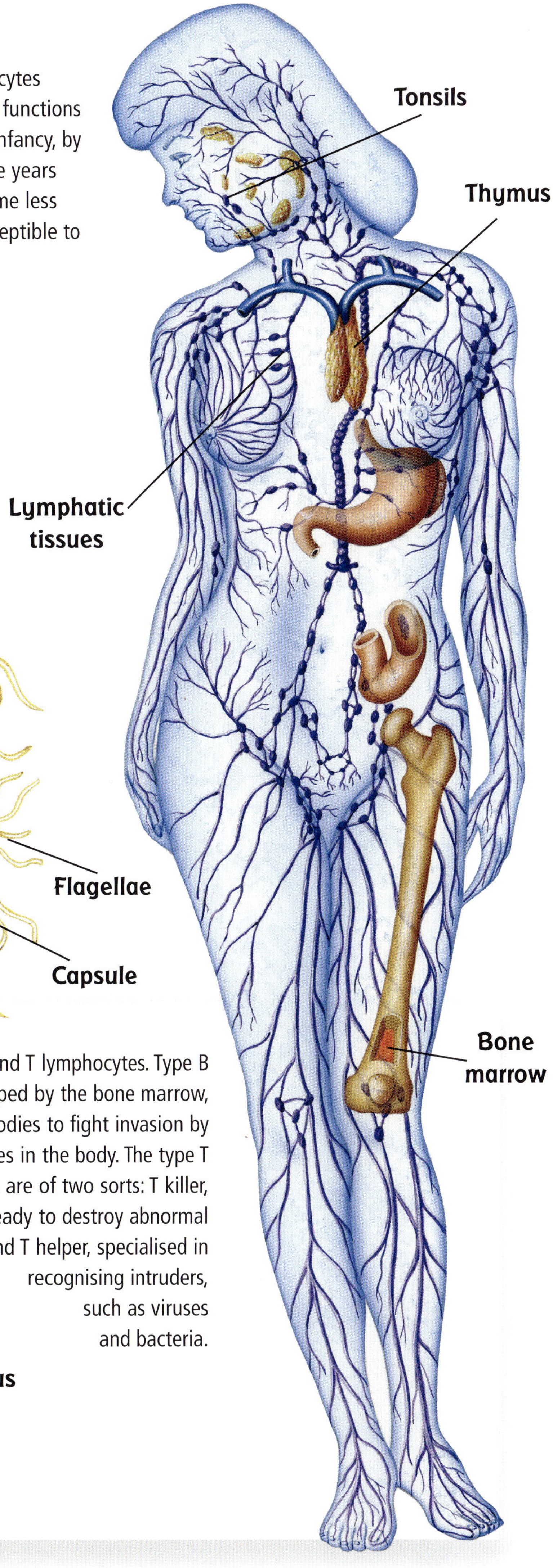

The lymphatic system does not have a pump to facilitate circulation. In the blood's circulatory system this work is performed by the heart, assisted by muscle movement. The rhythmic movement of the diaphragm and contraction of the vessels contribute to propel lymph through the body.

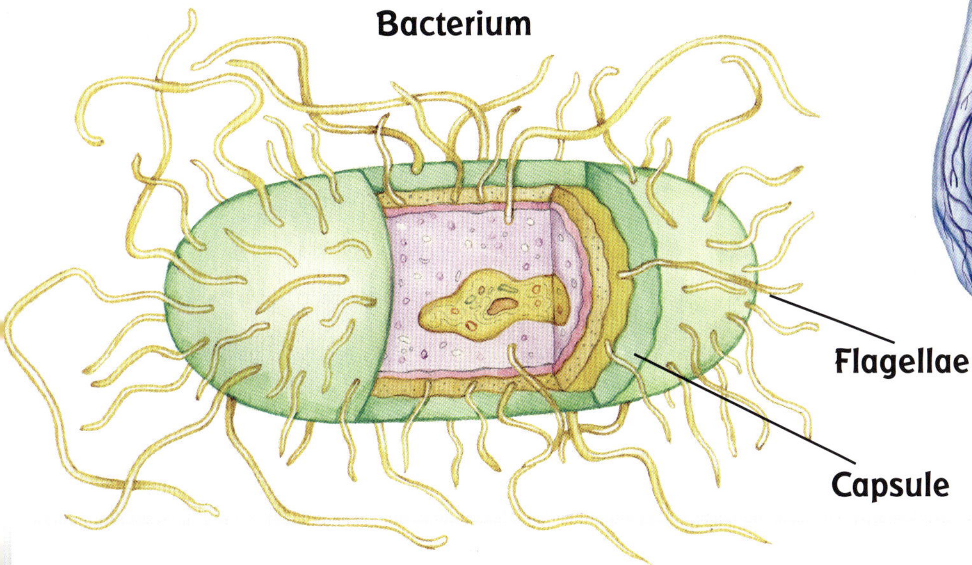

In our immune system there are types B and T lymphocytes. Type B lymphocytes, generated and developed by the bone marrow, specialise in producing antibodies to fight invasion by foreign molecules in the body. The type T lymphocytes are of two sorts: T killer, which are ready to destroy abnormal cells, and T helper, specialised in recognising intruders, such as viruses and bacteria.

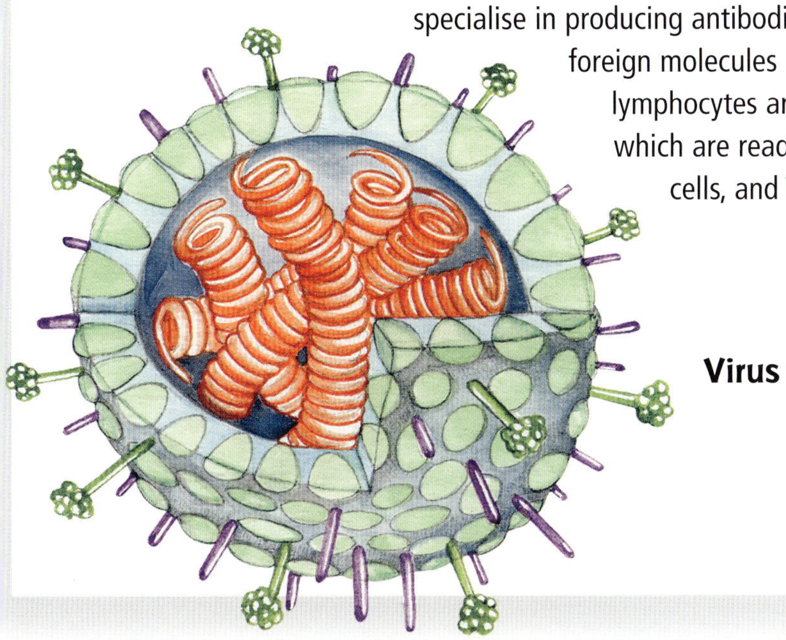

THE URINARY SYSTEM

The urinary system plays a very important purification role. It cleanses the body of waste produced by the cells during their normal activity. Urea and creatinine are the main toxic substances that are formed and need to be eliminated. In one day, the whole of the blood in the circulation is filtered around 300 times by two organs, the kidneys. Combined with the production of around one and a half litres of urine, this constant filtration process guarantees an effective cleansing system for our body.

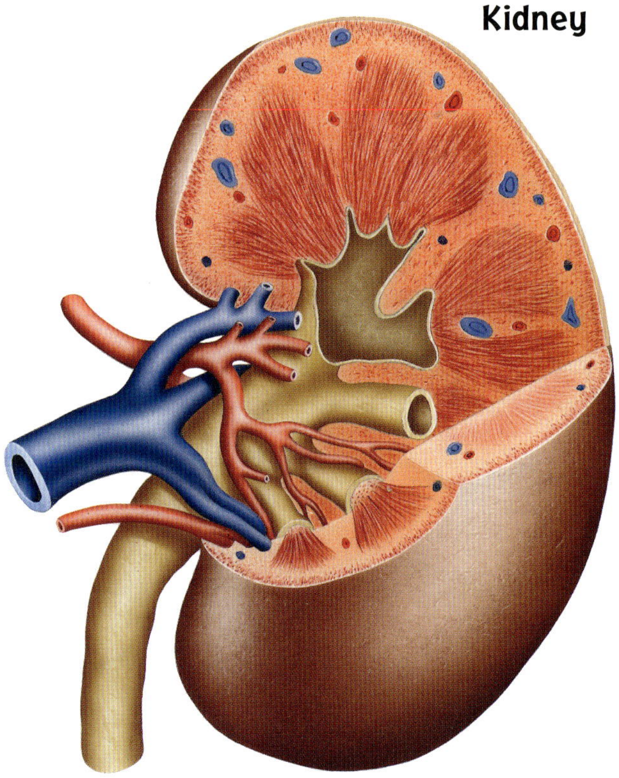

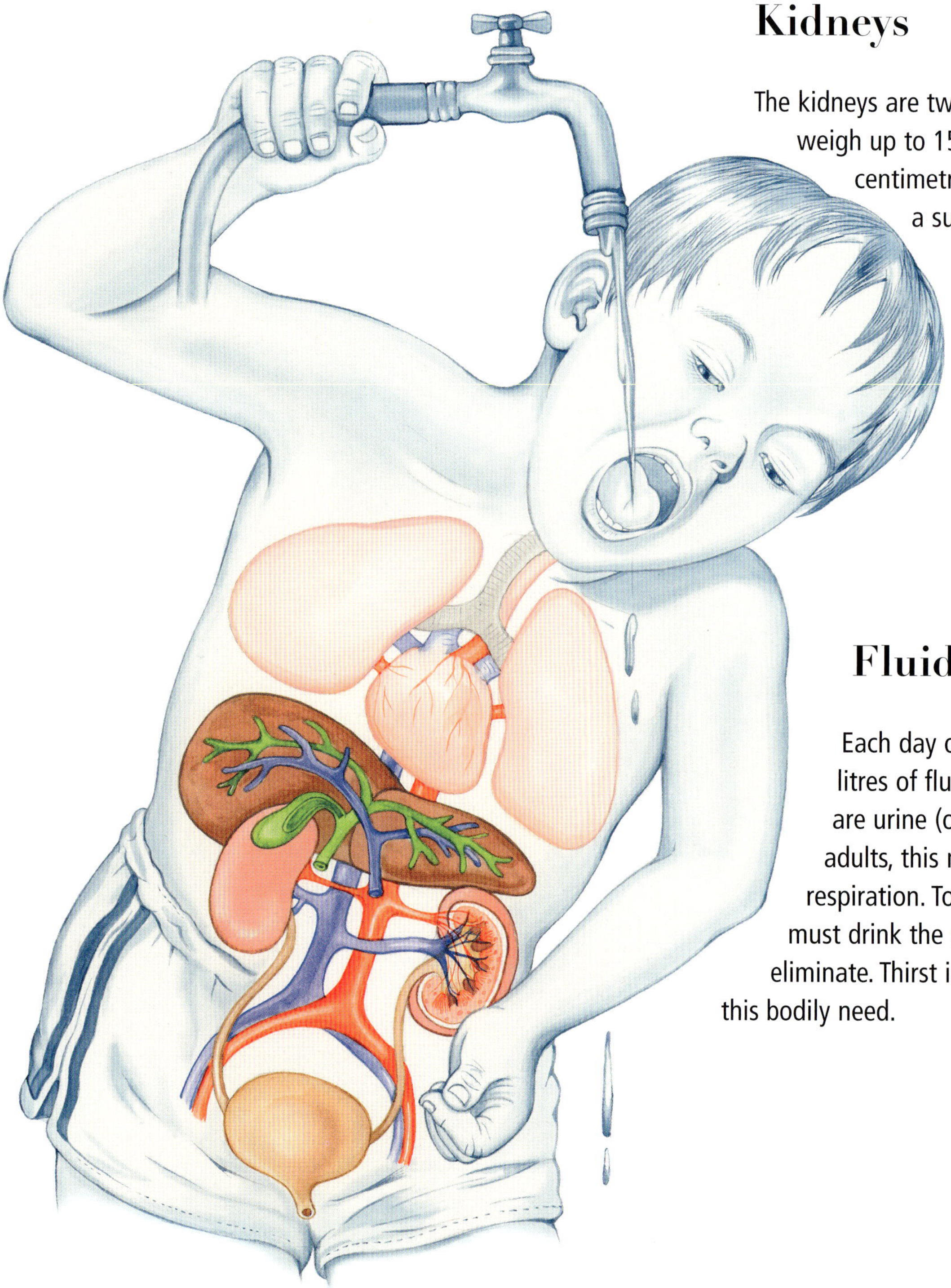

Kidneys

The kidneys are twin bean-shaped organs. In adults they weigh up to 150 or 160 grams, and measure about 12 centimetres in length. Despite their size, they have a surprising filtration capacity. The two renal arteries carry more than one litre of blood per minute to the kidneys. However, purification is not the only role played by the kidneys; they also ensure that our body is properly hydrated, by controlling the quantity of sodium in the blood.

Fluids

Each day our body loses between two and three litres of fluid. The main causes for this fluid loss are urine (one and a half litres), perspiration (in adults, this may amount to one litre per day) and respiration. To maintain effective hydration, we must drink the same quantity of water as we eliminate. Thirst is an important signal to remind us of this bodily need.

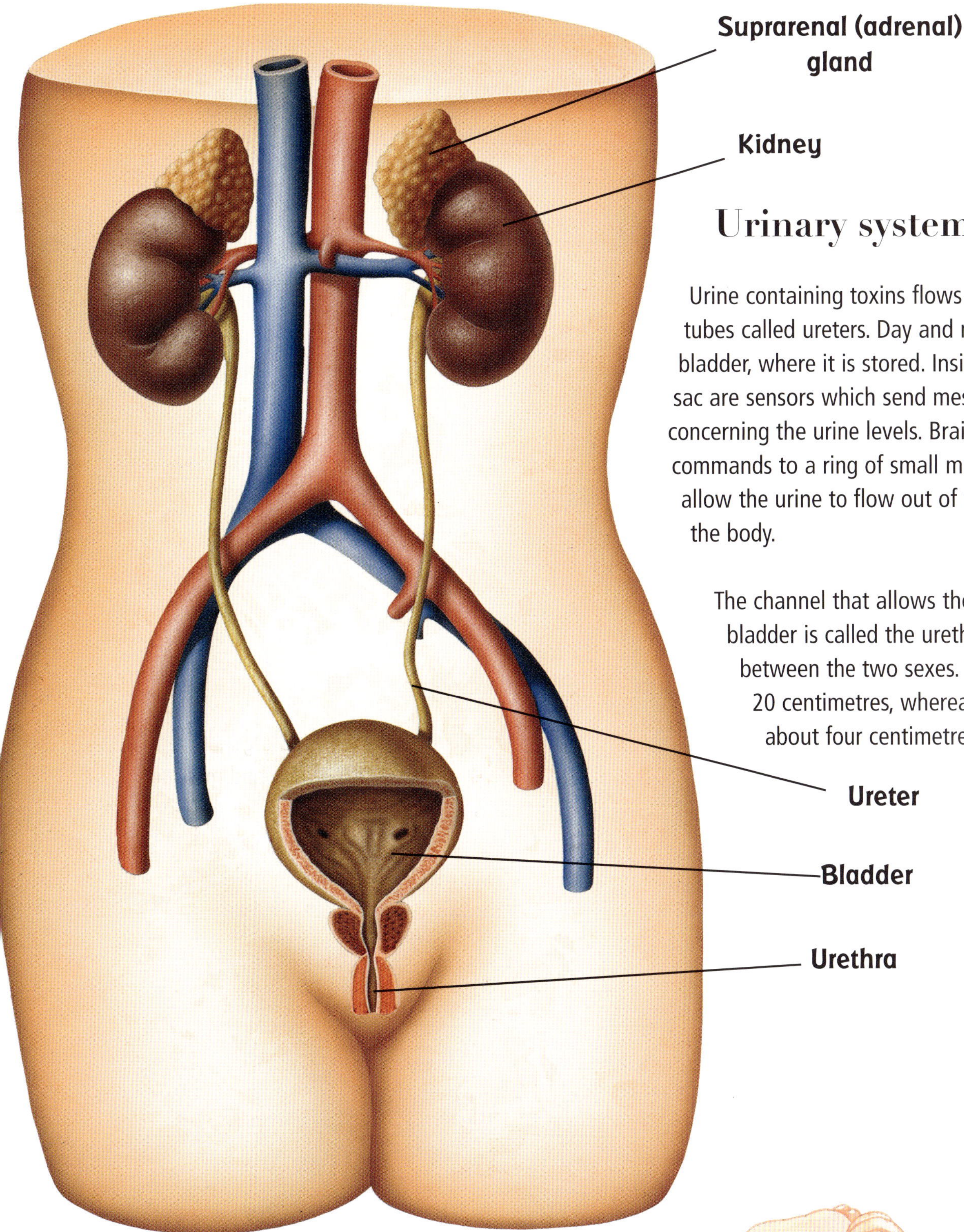

Urinary system

Urine containing toxins flows from the kidneys via two tubes called ureters. Day and night it flows into the bladder, where it is stored. Inside this flexible, watertight sac are sensors which send messages to the brain concerning the urine levels. Brain impulses send commands to a ring of small muscles which open and allow the urine to flow out of the bladder to outside the body.

The channel that allows the urine to escape from the bladder is called the urethra. Its length is variable between the two sexes. In men it measures around 20 centimetres, whereas in women it is only about four centimetres long.

When the urine level in the bladder reaches about 150 millilitres, we begin to feel the first urge to urinate.

In actual fact, we are able to 'hold on' to about twice that amount without any difficulty at all. Adults can control the urge to urinate for some time, whereas small children urinate at the first urge. As their nerve centres mature, at around two years of age, they develop better bladder control.

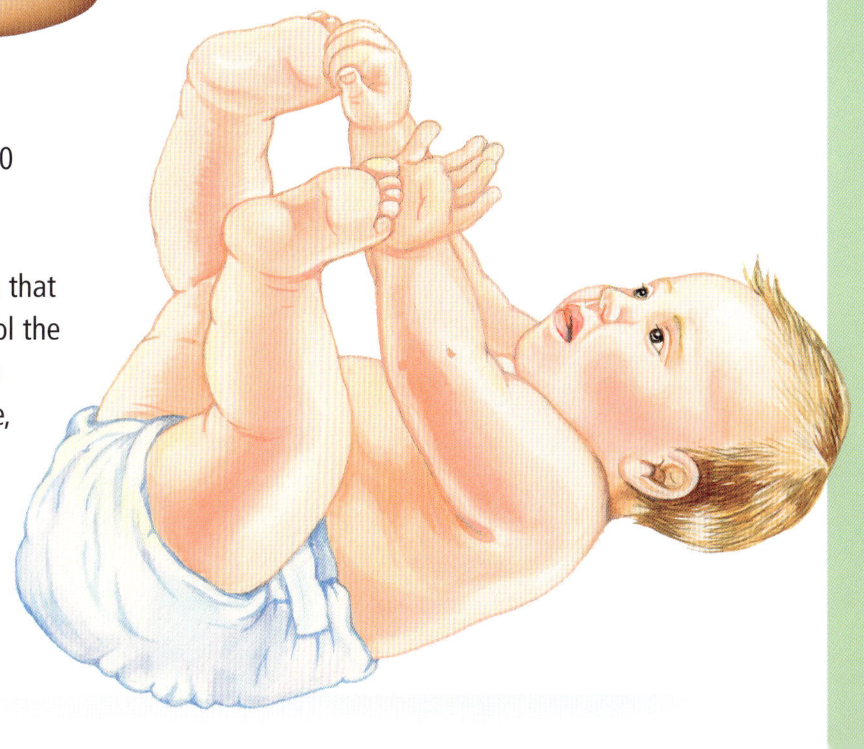

THE MALE REPRODUCTIVE SYSTEM

The male reproductive system comprises the organs which produce gametes, known as sperm, and which convey them inside the female sex organs. It consists of the external part containing two glands, called testicles, as well as the penis, which is the organ used during sexual intercourse. The testicles are located below the abdomen, and they produce sperm. Inside the male body are other glands which are also involved in the production of fluids which transport sperm. These are the prostate and the urethral glands. These seminal fluids (semen) reach the penis via the urethra.

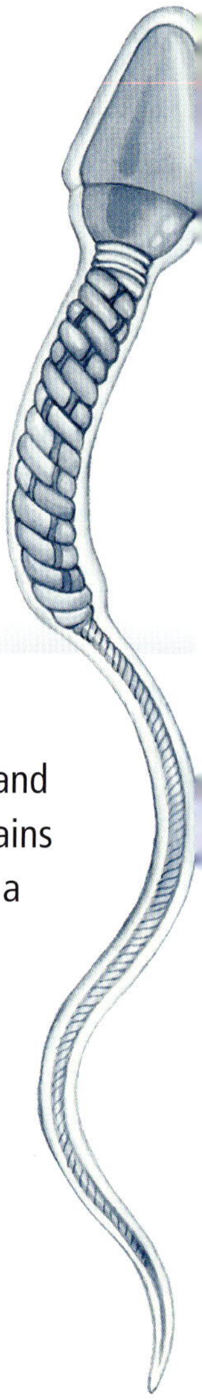

Sperm

The male sex cells (sperm) are long and tapered. The first part, or head, contains the genetic material. On the head is a sac filled with enzymes which are able to penetrate the outside layer of the egg. The central part is rich in mitochondria, which provide the energy necessary for sperm motility. The tail propels the spermatozoa along in their journey towards the ovum.

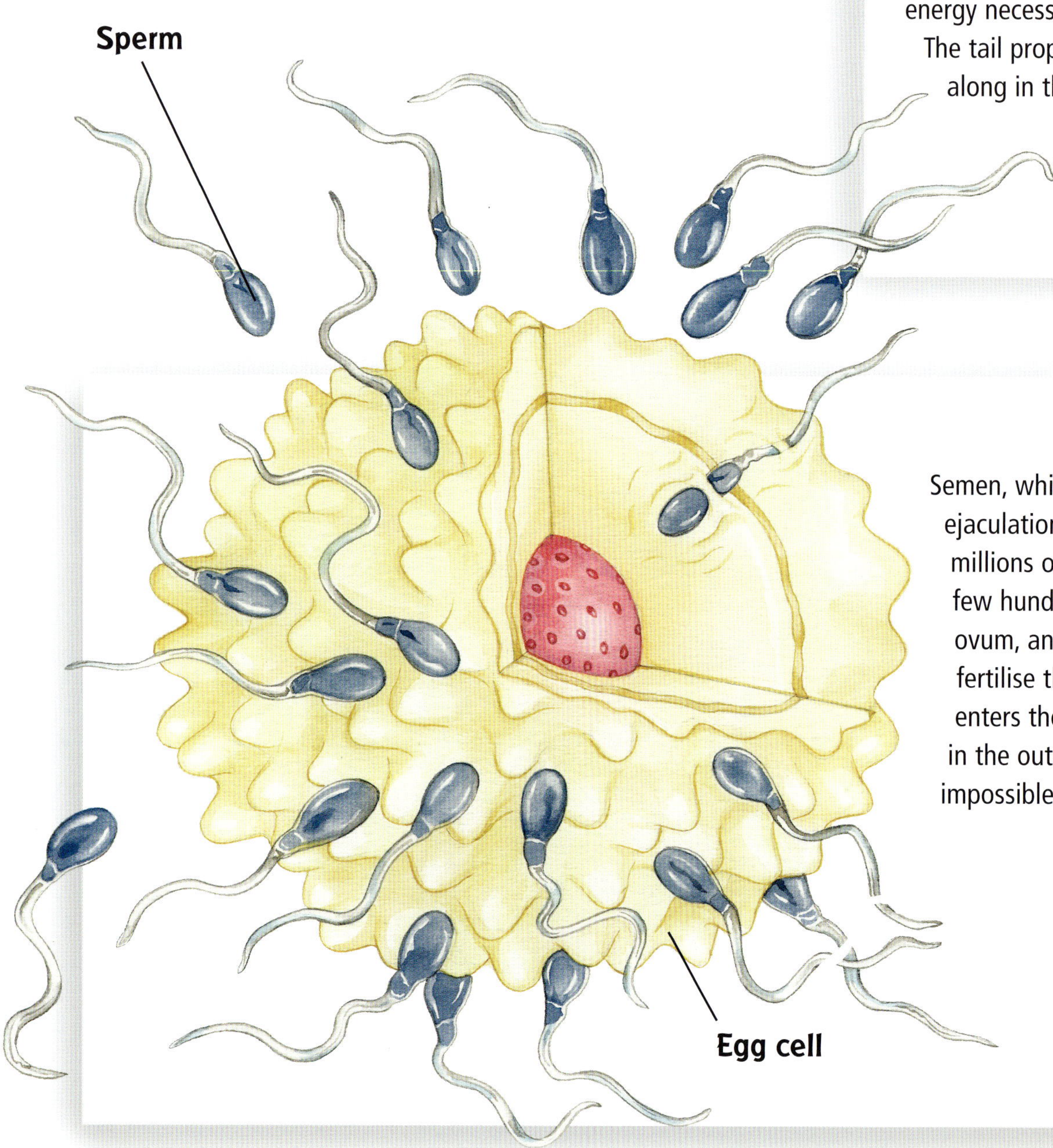

Semen, which is released during ejaculation, contains hundreds of millions of sperm. Of these, only a few hundred will reach the female ovum, and only one will manage to fertilise the egg. Once a single sperm enters the egg cell, a change occurs in the outside membrane, making it impossible for others to penetrate.

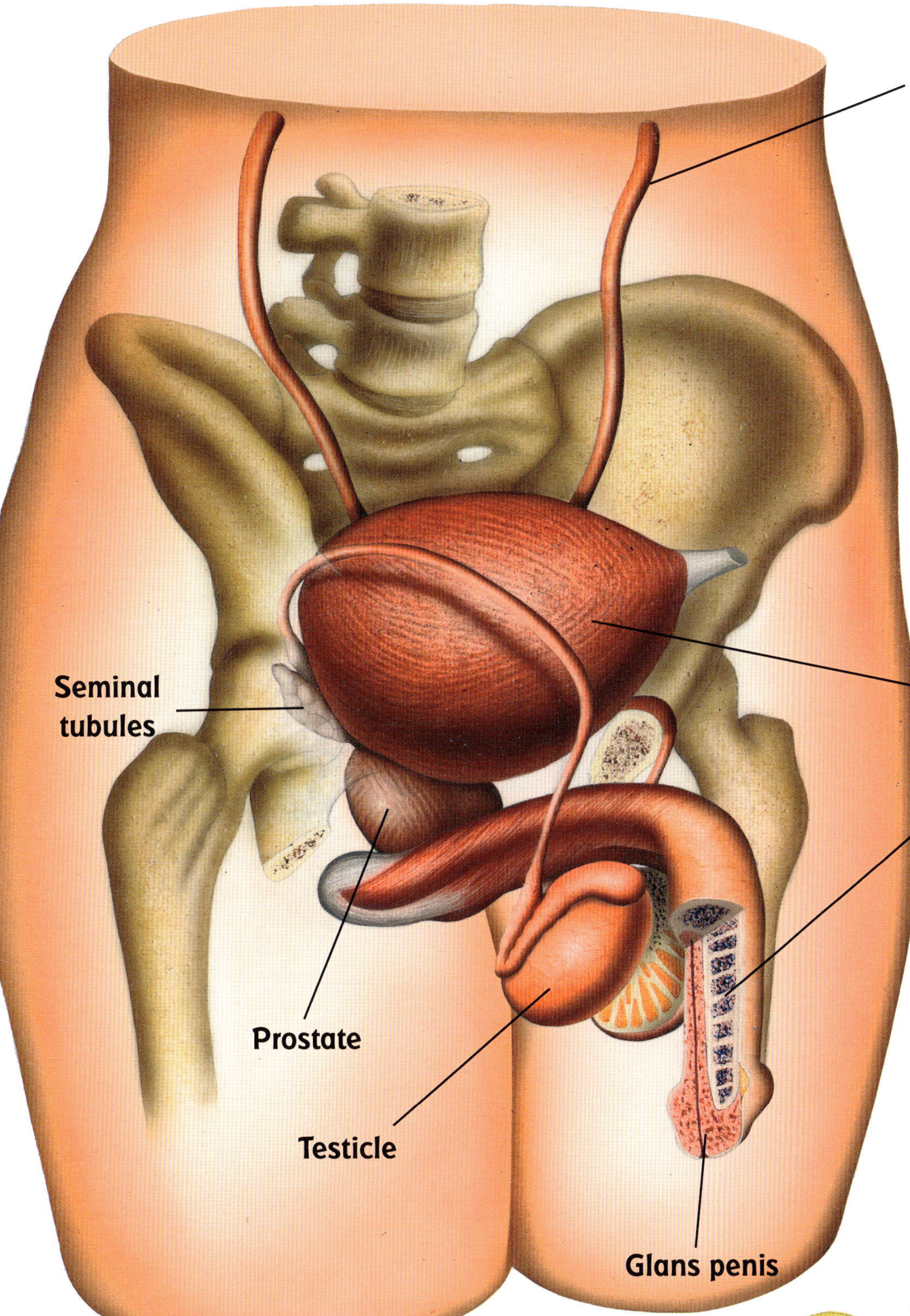

Fertilisation

At the climax of the sexual act of love-making, ejaculation occurs. Ejaculation causes the man's sperm to be expelled from the penis and deposited inside the woman's vagina. This is the start of the sperms' long journey towards the female egg.

A sperm takes about 65 days to develop. Following the first stage when it is formed inside the testicle, the cells are then stored in a duct called the epididymis. Each day, many hundreds of millions of spermatozoa are produced.

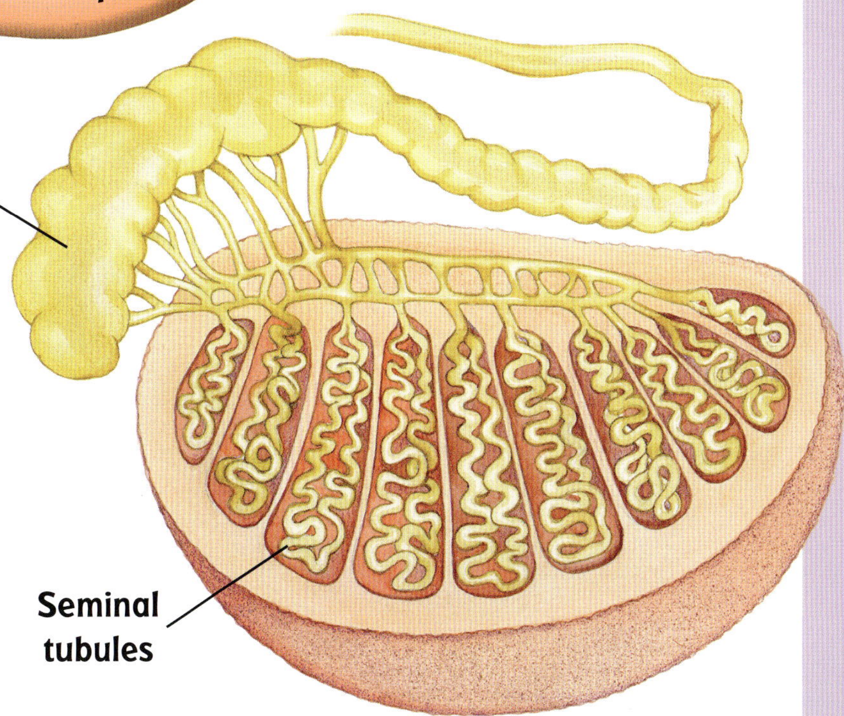

Testes

Spermatozoa are produced in the testicles, which are two glands located in a pouch located below the abdomen. The testicles (testes) are crisscrossed with tiny tubes called seminal tubules, where the formation of the sperm begins. The special cells forming the walls of these small tubes are responsible for creating the sperm.

THE FEMALE REPRODUCTIVE SYSTEM

The female reproductive system consists of the two ovaries which produce eggs cells, as well as the vagina and the uterus, which receive the male sperm and shelter the fertilised eggs. All the female organs are internal, and only the vaginal opening is visible outside the body.

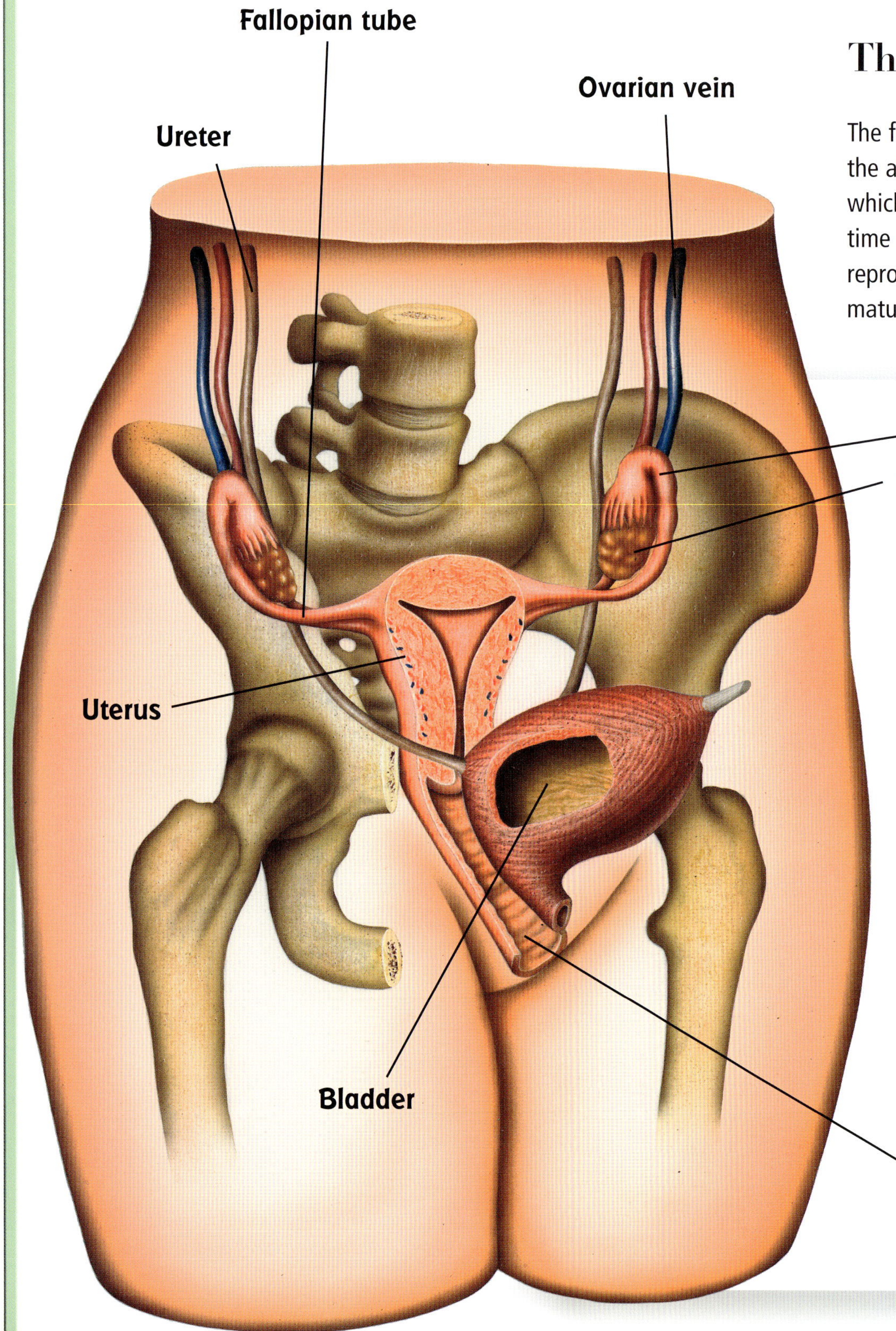

The ovaries

The female gonads are located on either side of the abdominal cavity. They contain egg cells which are present in a woman's body from the time she is born. During the woman's reproductive life approximately 400 eggs will mature and await fertilisation.

Menstruation

All throughout her reproductive life a woman has menstrual cycles. The organs of the reproductive system undergo cyclical changes, which adapt to the different phases of maturation of the egg cell and its eventual shedding if it has not been fertilised. At around the time of ovulation, the lining of the uterus thickens with a tissue rich in blood vessels and prepares to receive the fertilised egg. If fertilisation does not occur, this tissue dies and is expelled from the body, causing a small haemorrhage known as a 'period', or menstruation.

Ovulation

When an egg cell is mature, the follicle which envelops it opens and releases it from the ovary. The egg begins its journey down a duct known as a Fallopian tube, on its way to the uterus. The period during this journey is the best time for fertilisation to occur.

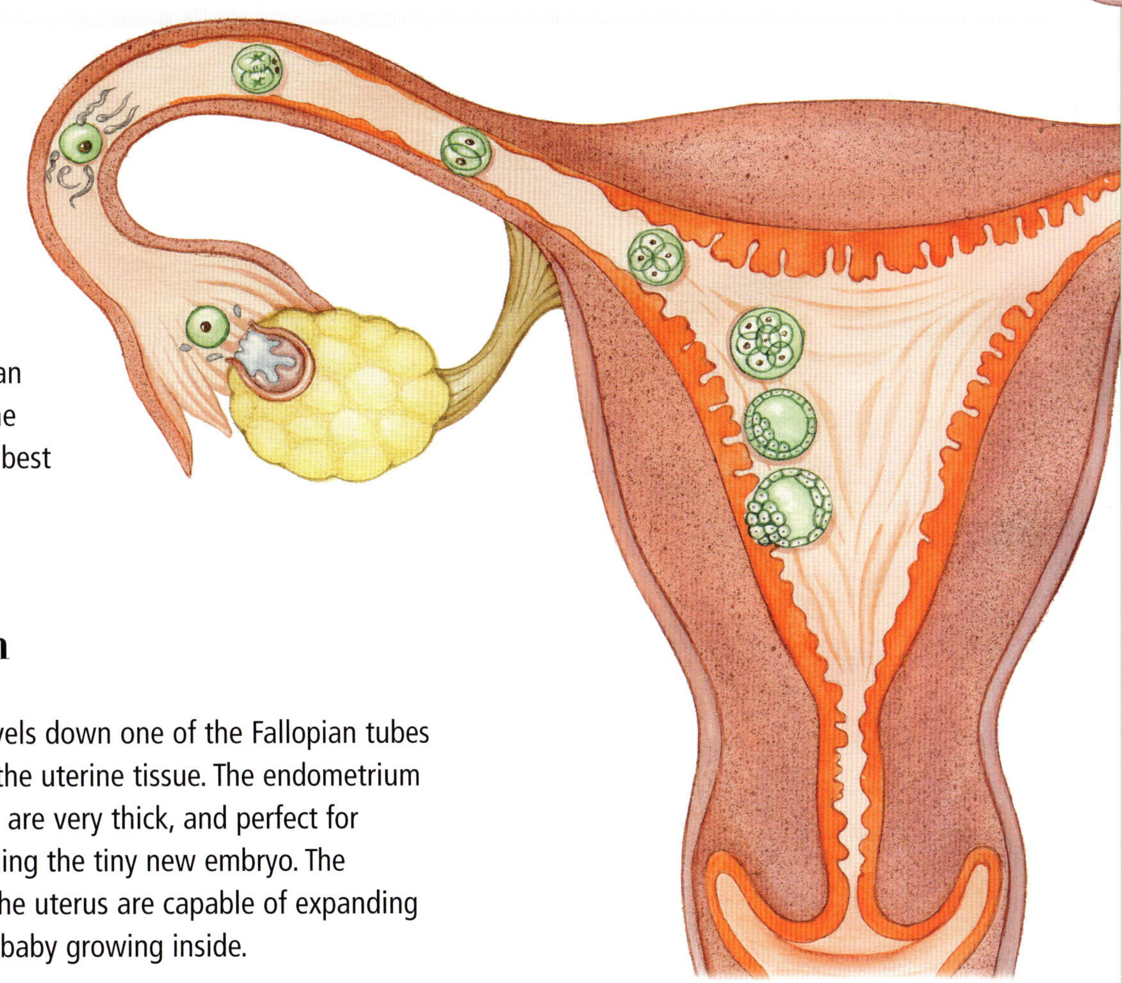

Fertilisation

The fertilised egg travels down one of the Fallopian tubes and embeds itself in the uterine tissue. The endometrium or walls of this organ are very thick, and perfect for receiving and nourishing the tiny new embryo. The muscle layers lining the uterus are capable of expanding to accommodate the baby growing inside.

The menstrual cycle is repeated every 28 days. During this interval, the egg cell matures and is shed by the ovary on around the 14th day. At the same time, during the first five days of the menstrual cycle, the uterus sheds its old endometrium, and on the sixth day the new lining starts to form. About 14 days after ovulation, if fertilisation does not occur, the endometrium begins to break down and the next menstrual period begins.

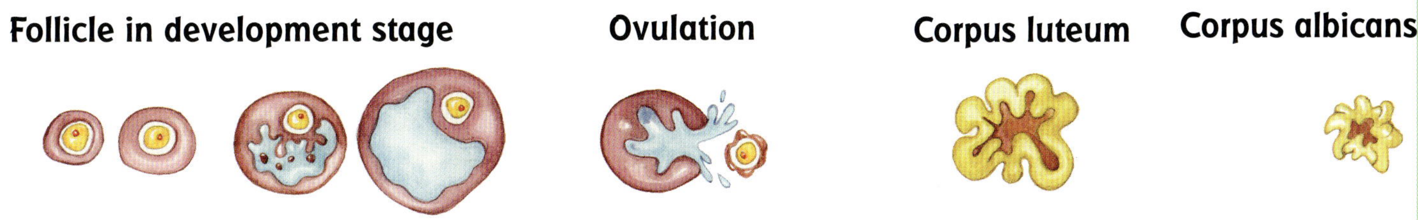

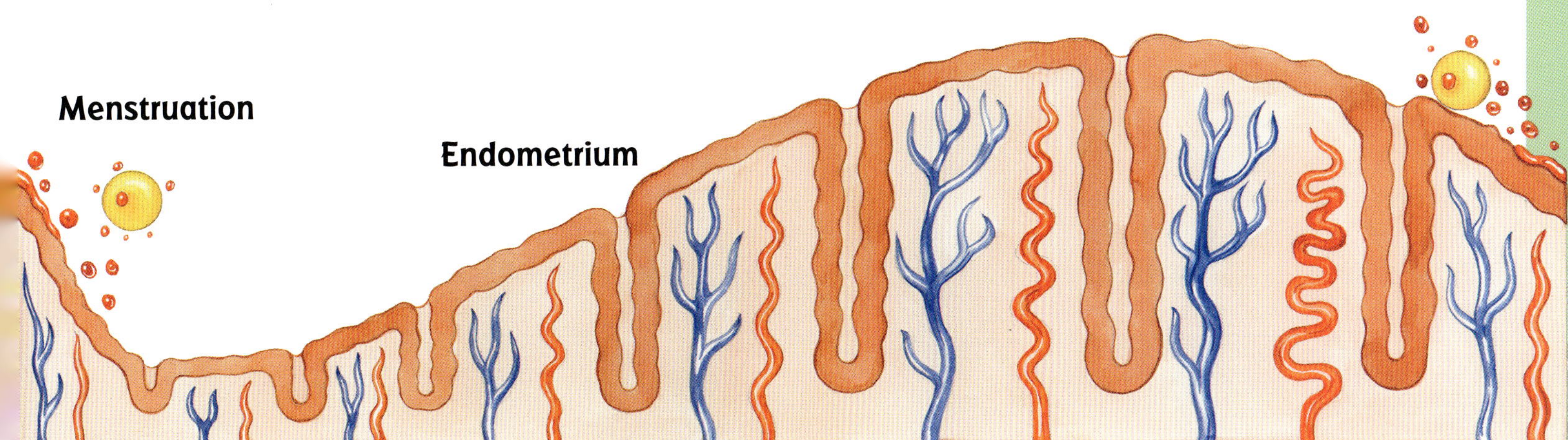

GESTATION

The fertilised egg is implanted in the uterus and begins to receive nourishment from the mother. The embryo starts to develop very quickly. At three weeks gestation, the brain and spinal cord are visible. At the end of the second month all the vital organs are formed. Up to this stage the embryo is very small, but it already has a human shape and we can just make out the budding facial features. The third month is the beginning of the stage when the weight of the baby increases rapidly, from about 30 grams to one kilogram in the seventh month of pregnancy. By that stage, the baby could survive outside the mother's uterus, but only with the help of special equipment. Over the next two months fetal development is completed, and both mother and infant are preparing for the birth.

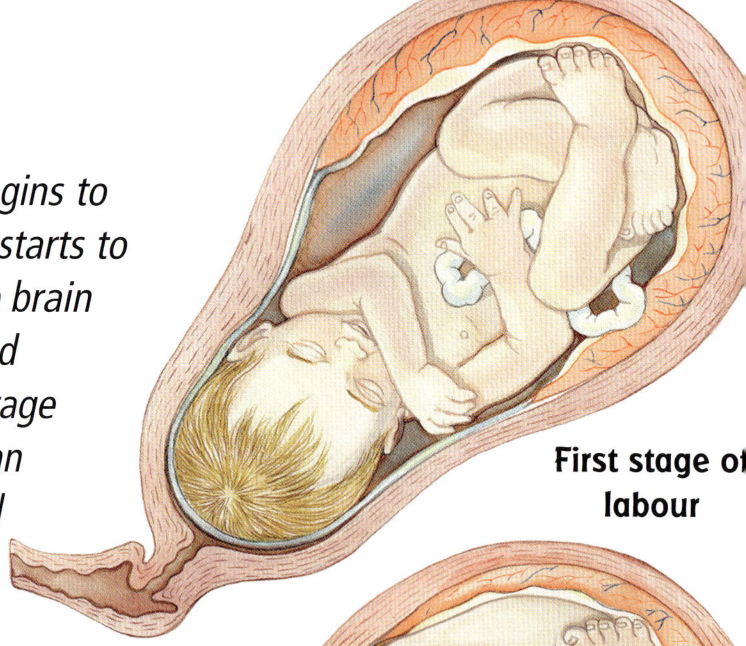

First stage of labour

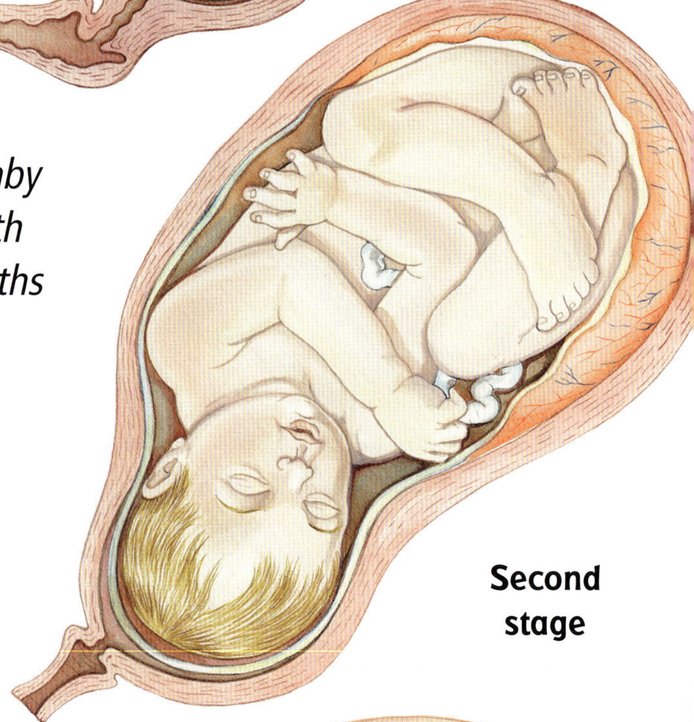

Second stage

Labour

Pregnancy in the human female lasts for approximately nine months, culminating in childbirth. The fetus prepares for the birth by moving downwards towards the vagina, and at the same time a specific hormone triggers pain, announcing the onset of the stage known as labour. During this period the muscles of the uterine wall begin to contract rhythmically, becoming gradually more intense and more frequent. The cervix dilates to allow the baby's head to begin its journey into the outside world. These uterine contractions are the final stage of labour before the newborn is expelled from the mother's body. Usually the baby arrives headfirst, and the rest of the body follows very easily. During the different stages of labour, the baby remains connected to the placenta by the umbilical cord, which is cut as soon as the baby is able to breathe unassisted.

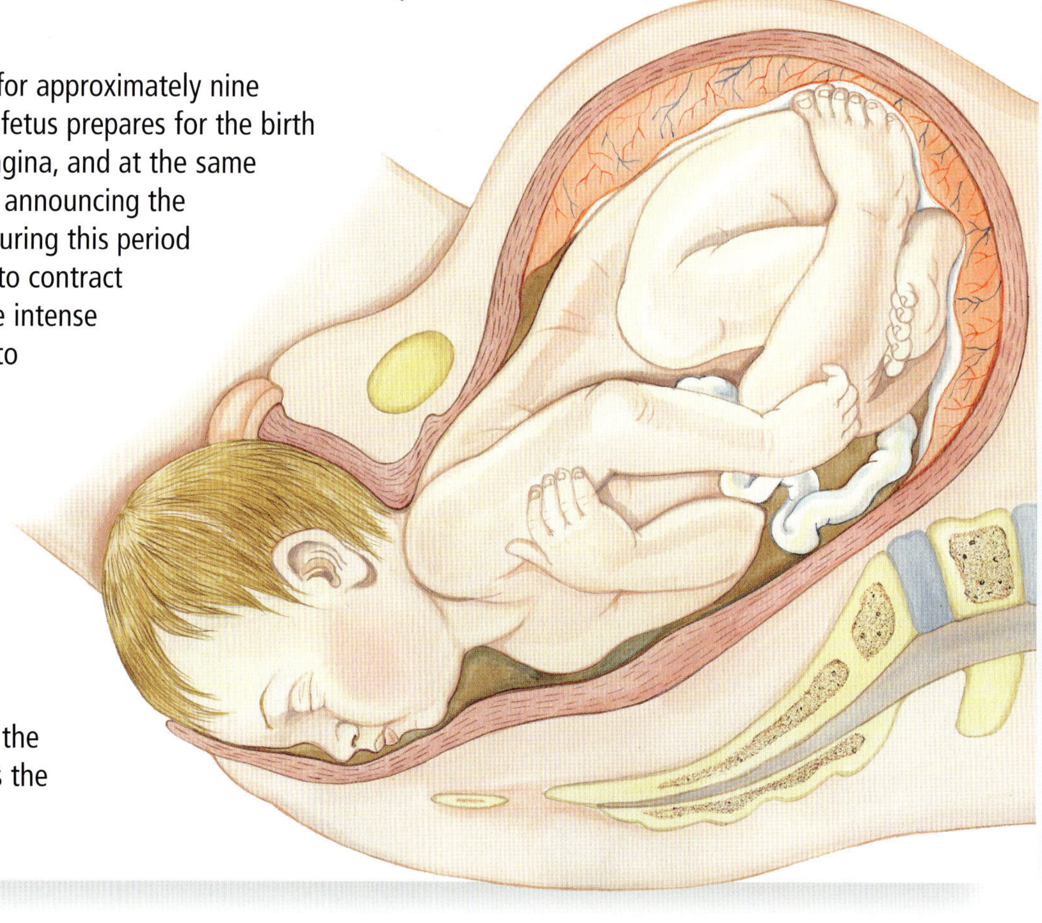

Breastfeeding

Immediately following birth, the infant is able to suck milk from the mother's breast. All newborn mammals have this suckling instinct. Mother's milk is most important for infants because it is highly nourishing and provides valuable antibodies that protect them from disease.

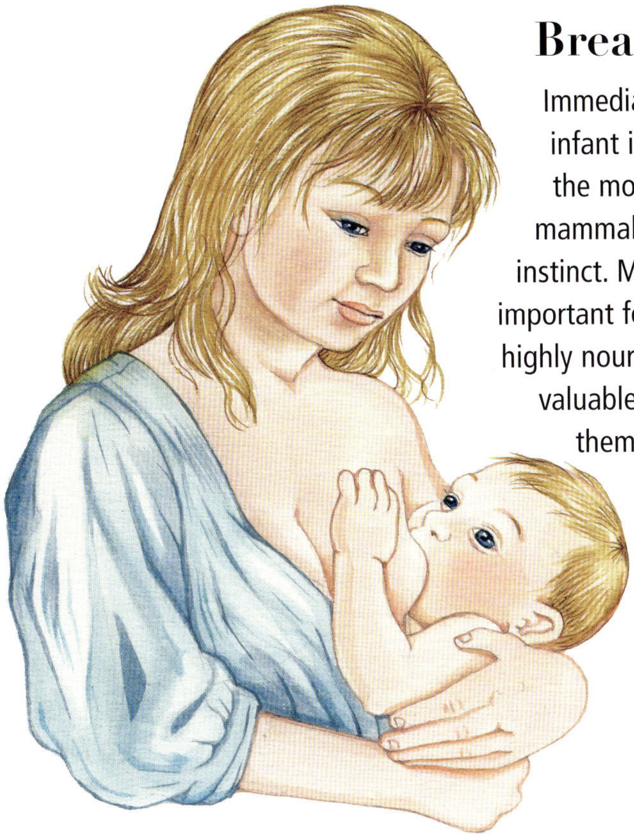

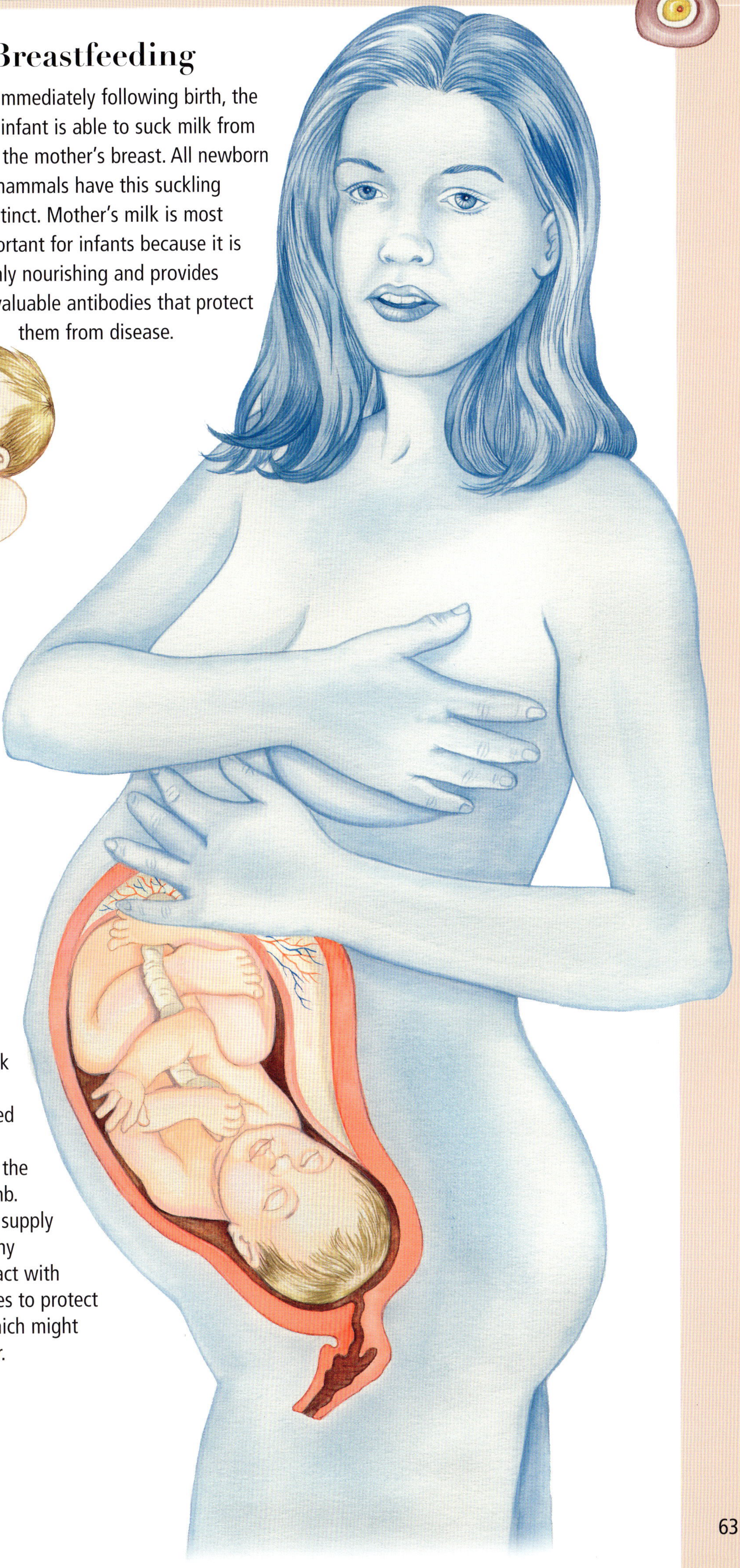

The breast

The mammary glands are formed from little rounded lobes. Inside these lobes are even smaller lobules where milk is produced soon after birth.

The placenta

As soon as the fertilised ovum attaches itself inside the uterus, it begins to be irrigated by the mother's blood, via small capillaries. Gradually, a very dense network of blood vessels forms a kind of pouch around the fetus. This vascular organ, called the placenta, performs the work of the intestine, the lungs and the kidneys while the infant is growing inside the mother's womb. Through the placenta, the mother's blood supply provides all that the fetus needs for healthy development, yet without any direct contact with the baby's blood. This natural barrier serves to protect the infant from a number of infections which might otherwise be transmitted from the mother.

INDEX

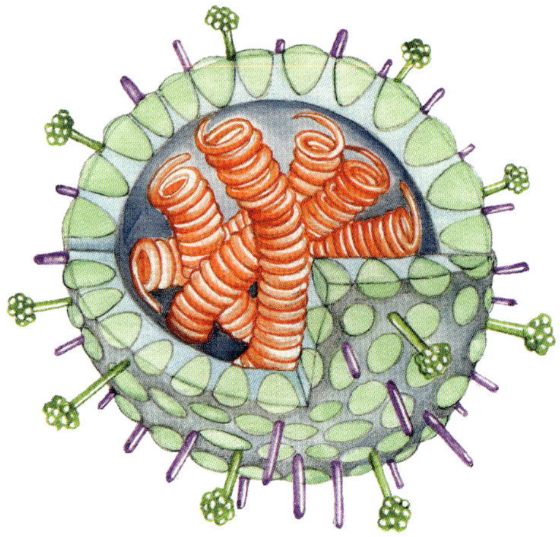

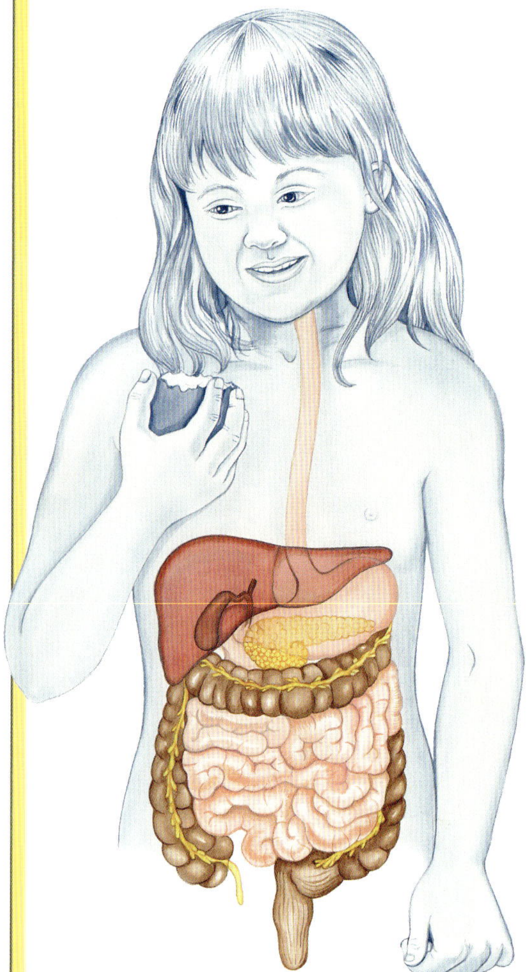

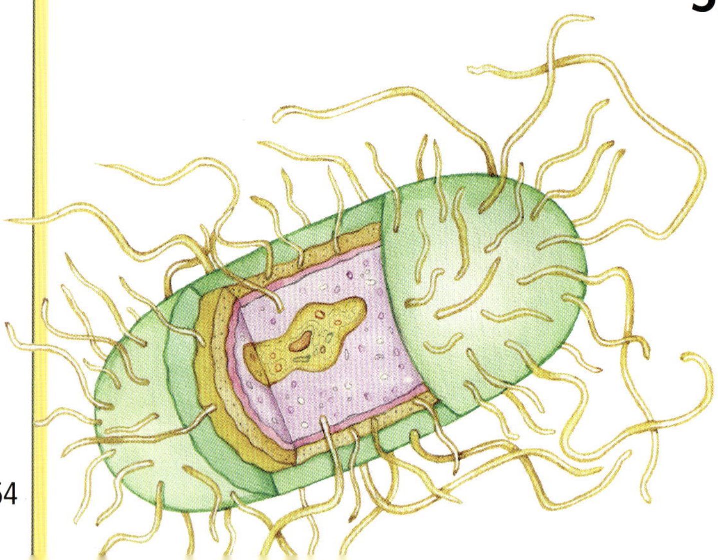

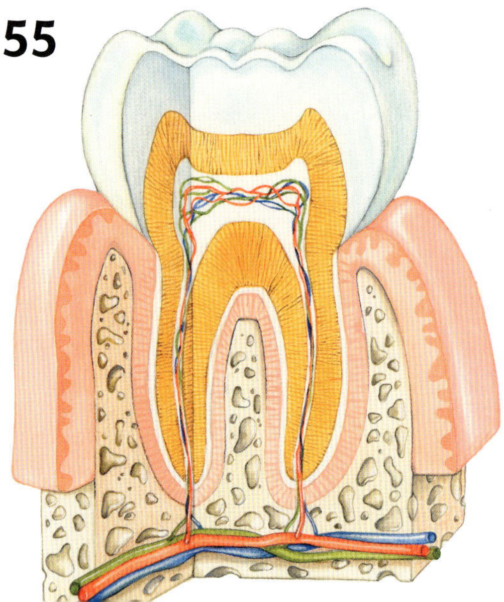

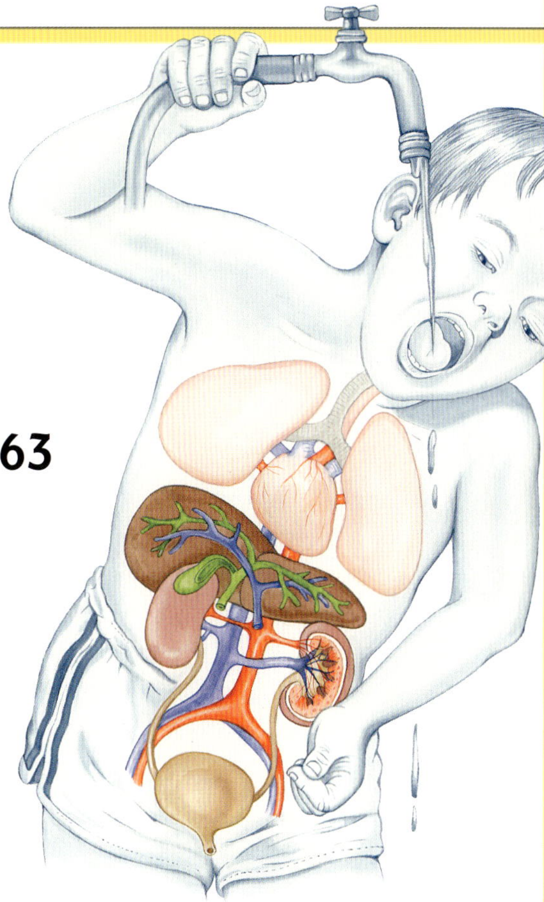

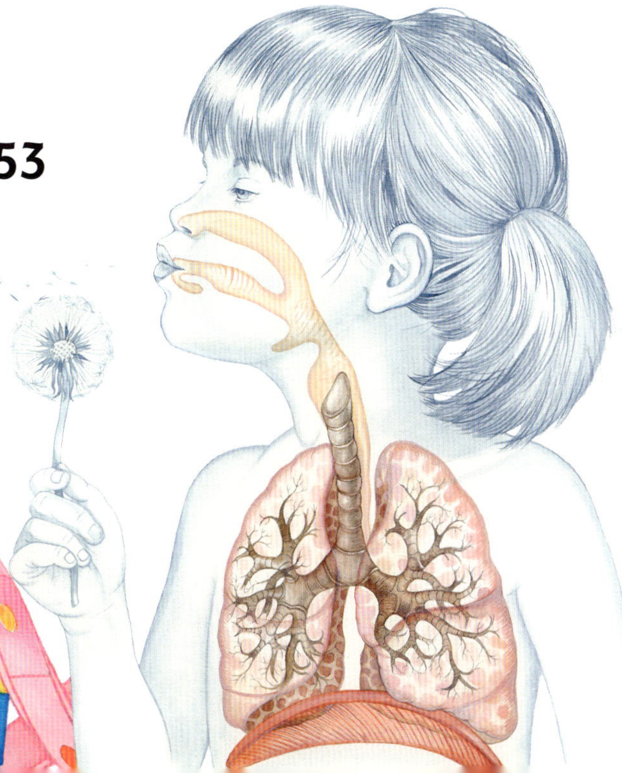

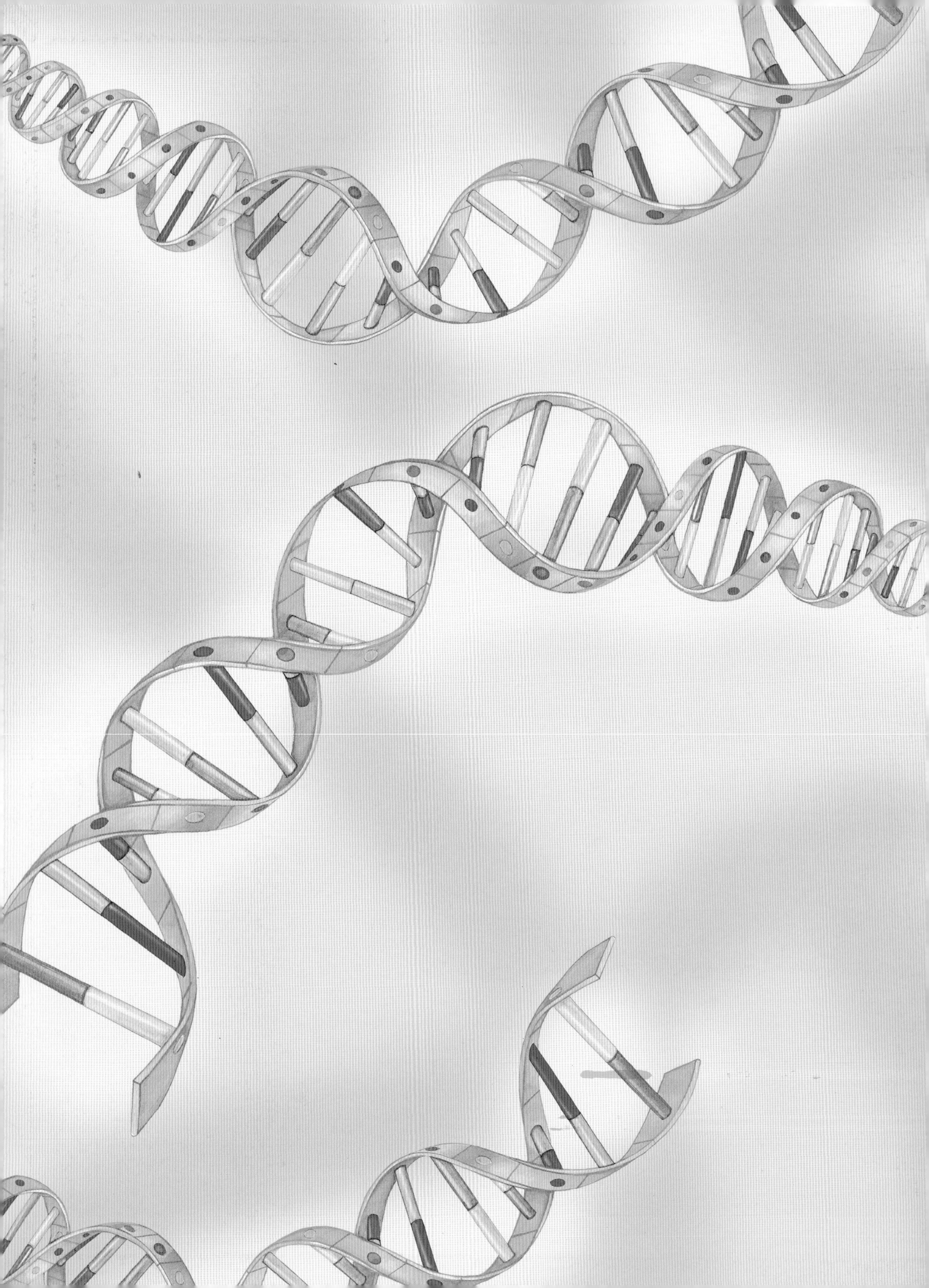